Machine Learning

Machine learning is a dynamic and rapidly expanding field focused on creating algorithms that empower computers to recognize patterns, make predictions and continually enhance performance. It enables computers to learn from data and experiences, making decisions without explicit programming. For learners, mastering the fundamentals of machine learning opens doors to a world of possibilities to build robust and accurate models. In the ever-evolving landscape of machine learning, datasets play a pivotal role in shaping its future. The field has been revolutionized with the introduction of oneAPI, which provides a unified programming model across different architectures, including CPUs, GPUs, FPGAs and accelerators, fostering an efficient and portable programming environment. Embracing this unified model empowers practitioners to build efficient and scalable machine learning solutions, marking a significant stride in cross-architecture development. Dive into this fascinating field to master machine learning concepts with the step-by-step approach outlined in this book and contribute to its exciting future.

T0351300

Machine Learning
A Comprehensive Beginner's Guide

Akshay B R, Sini Raj Pulari,
T S Murugesh, and
Shriram K Vasudevan

CRC Press
Taylor & Francis Group
Boca Raton London New York

CRC Press is an imprint of the
Taylor & Francis Group, an **informa** business

Designed cover image: Shutterstock Images

First edition published 2025
by CRC Press
2385 NW Executive Center Drive, Suite 320, Boca Raton FL 33431

and by CRC Press
4 Park Square, Milton Park, Abingdon, Oxon, OX14 4RN

CRC Press is an imprint of Taylor & Francis Group, LLC

© 2025 Akshay B R, Sini Raj Pulari, T S Murugesh, and Shriram K Vasudevan

ISBN: 978-1-032-67665-4 (hbk)
ISBN: 978-1-032-67666-1 (pbk)
ISBN: 978-1-032-67668-5 (ebk)

DOI: 10.1201/9781032676685

Typeset in Sabon
by Newgen Publishing UK

Contents

Preface

Machine learning is an exciting and rapidly growing field which is all about creating algorithms and models that enable computers to recognize patterns, make predictions, and improve their performance over time. It empowers computers to learn from data and experiences and make decisions without being explicitly programmed. For beginners, understanding the fundamentals of machine learning can open doors to a world of possibilities. Machine learning is as effective as the datasets it relies on. By understanding the nuances of different types of datasets, conducting thorough exploration, and following best practices, practitioners can harness the power of data to build robust and accurate machine learning models. As the field continues to advance, the role of datasets in shaping the future of machine learning becomes increasingly pivotal.

Machine learning (ML) has revolutionized various industries, and with the advent of oneAPI, the landscape has evolved even further. oneAPI simplifies the development process by providing a unified programming model that spans different architectures, including CPUs, GPUs, FPGAs, and accelerators. It aims to break down the barriers between traditional and specialized computing, fostering a more efficient and portable programming environment. By embracing a unified programming model, oneAPI also empowers practitioners to build efficient and scalable machine learning solutions, marking a significant stride in the evolution of cross-architecture development.

Embarking on the journey of machine learning as a beginner may seem daunting, but with a step-by-step approach followed in this book, it becomes an accessible and rewarding endeavor. You can delve into this fascinating field, to master machine learning concepts.

Authors

Akshay B R, a final-year BTech computer science engineering student and an Intel student ambassador, is a passionate data science enthusiast. He primarily works on problems involving disease prediction and developing healthcare systems. He has published multiple articles in a variety of top journals and conferences. He is also a freelance machine learning tutor and has trained around 2000+ students.

Sini Raj Pulari is Professor and Tutor currently working at the Government University (Bahrain Polytechnic, Faculty of EDICT) in the Kingdom of Bahrain. She has 16 years of teaching experience at various Indian universities and in industry, contributing to the teaching field and carrying out activities to maintain and develop research and professional activities relevant to computer science engineering. Her research interests include natural language processing, recommender systems, information retrieval, deep learning, and machine learning. She has authored more than 20 Scopus Indexed Publications and co-authored *Deep Learning: A Comprehensive Guide* (CRC Press/Taylor & Francis). Sini has developed and guided more than 40 undergraduate and postgraduate projects, and she is an active member of boards of curriculum development for various universities. Sini has delivered more than 40 invited lectures on applications and emerging trends in a variety of technological and research advancements. She was a speaker at the workshops AI for All, Understanding Deep Learning Algorithms – Convolution Neural Networks with Real Time Applications, Using Python, Keras and Tensor Flow. She has also participated in the MENA Hackathon group discussion on "innovating tech-based solutions for challenges in the healthcare and energy, environment and sustainability sectors," which was in partnership with Tamkeen, powered by Amazon Web Services (AWS) and Elijah Coaching and Consulting Services. Sini has completed various certifications such as Apple Certified Trainer, SCJP, Oracle Certified Associate, APQMR-Quality Matters, etc.

T S Murugesh has 24 years of experience in academia in the fields of analog and digital electronics, automation and control, IoT, system design, image processing, artificial intelligence, machine learning, instrumentation, and computational bio-engineering. After a tenure of 19 years with the Department of Electronics and Instrumentation Engineering, Faculty of Engineering and Technology, Annamalai University, Tamil Nadu, India, he is an Associate Professor in the Department of Electronics and Communication Engineering, Government College of Engineering, Srirangam, Tiruchirappalli, Tamil Nadu, India. He has delivered several talks at international conferences and given more than two dozen invited lectures at the national level at various institutions, including Sastra University, Annamalai University, Mahatma Gandhi University, Kerala, National Institute of Technology, Tiruchirappalli, etc. He has 50+ peer-reviewed indexed papers in journals, including Springer, Springer Nature, Elsevier, Wiley, Inderscience, etc. He has organized faculty development programs at the national level, and he is a reviewer for IEEE, Inderscience and many other peer-reviewed journals. He has coauthored five books for CRC Press/Taylor & Francis (UK) and is currently co-authoring a book for Nova Science Publishers, USA and two books for CRC Press.

Dr. Murugesh has donned the role of Mentor, Primary Evaluator for the Government of India's Smart India Hackathon 2022, Toycathon2021, Judge in the Grand Finale in Toycathon 2021, evaluator in The Kavach2023 Cybersecurity Hackathon, organized by the Ministry of Home Affairs (MHA) in collaboration with the Ministry of Education's (MoE) Innovation Cell, Government of India. He is a hackathon enthusiast, and his team has won first prize in the CloudFest Hackathon 2 presented by Google Cloud, DigitalGov Hack, the Hackathon by WSIS Forum 2023 and Digital Government Authority, Saudi Arabia. His team has also won the MSME Idea Hackathon 2.0 and received 15 Lakhs funding from the Ministry of Micro, Small and Medium Enterprises (MSME) Innovative Scheme, Government of India, as well as the Second Prize in the IFGxTA Hub Hackathon 2022.

Dr. Murugesh is a certified Intel oneAPI Innovator, Mentor under the National Initiative for Technical Teachers Training programme from AICTE, and the National Institute of Technical Teachers Training and Research, and a Certified Microsoft Educator Academy Professional. He is also a Master Assessor for a Naan Mudhalvan Program, 2023, devised by the Government of Tamil Nadu, a reviewer of BE/BTech technical books in the regional language scheme of AICTE, coordinated by the Centre for Development of Tamil in Engineering and Technology, Anna University, Tamil Nadu, India. Huawei has recognized Dr. Murugesh for his academic collaboration. He is a Conference Committee Member, Publishing Committee Member of the International Association of Applied Science and Technology. He holds editorial board membership with the *American Journal of Embedded Systems and Applications*. He has also served as Technical Program Committee

Member for a Springer-sponsored, Scopus-Indexed International Conference conducted at Sharda University, India, and he is a Scientific Committee Member for an International Conference conducted at the Sultanate of Oman and a chairperson of an International Hybrid Conference at Mahatma Gandhi University Kerala, India. Dr. Murugesh has held various academic responsibilities, such as Chairman for Anna University Central Valuation, Chief Superintendent for the Anna University Theory Examinations, and the Exam Cell Coordinator for his institution. He also holds professional body membership in the Institution of Engineers (India).

Shriram K Vasudevan has more than 17 years of experience in industry and academia. He earned a PhD in embedded systems. He has authored or co-authored 45 books for various publishers, including Taylor & Francis, Oxford University Press, and Wiley. He also has been granted 13 patents so far. Shriram is a hackathon enthusiast and has been awarded by Harvard University, AICITE, CII, Google, TDRA Dubai, the Government of Saudi Arabia, the Government of India, and many more. He has published more than 150 research articles. He was associated with L&T Technology Services before joining Intel in a current role. Dr. Vasudevan operates a YouTube channel in his name, which has more than 41,000 subscribers and maintains a wide range of playlists on varied topics. He is a public speaker as well. Dr. Vasudevan is a oneAPI-Certified Instructor, Intel oneAPI-Certified Instructor, Google Cloud Ambassador, Streamlit Education Ambassador, AWS Ambassador, ACM Distinguished Speaker and NASSCOM Prime Ambassador. He is a Fellow IEI, Fellow IETE and Senior Member IEEE.

Introduction

What is Machine Learning?

LEARNING OBJECTIVES

After reading this chapter, the reader shall be able to understand the following:

- What is machine learning?
- Relationship between AL, ML, and DL
- What are the types of machine learning?
- Why do we need machine learning?
- The machine learning framework
- Machine learning vs. deep learning
- Machine learning applications

P1.1 INTRODUCTION

The term machine learning (ML) belonging to the research field of Artificial Intelligence (AI) has been buzzing around us for quite a few decades. Most of us would have already carried out some attempts to understand "what the word level abstract meaning is" at least by performing a google search. Even if you have not done that, do not worry you are at the right place to learn in depth about "What is machine learning?" in a technical perspective. The intention of this chapter does not stop there; yes, we will dive a little deeper to understand the various types of machine learning, its application in real-life scenarios, and the differences between ML and deep learning (DL).

P1.2 WHAT IS MACHINE LEARNING?

Okay, let us start by taking you back to your childhood. Do you remember how many times you fell before you started to walk properly? That's a pretty old memory for you to recollect – we should probably direct this question to your parents. Let us consider an example, which you might remember even

DOI: 10.1201/9781032676685-1

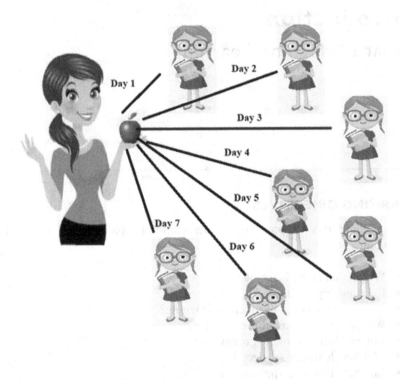

Figure P1.1 Teacher showing (training) the student for a week "what is an apple?".

now. Every one of us would have had a favorite Kindergarten teacher, who was so sweet and patient to you. Yes, I used the word patient intentionally. You know why! I still remember the way my Kindergarten teacher taught me what an apple is. She literarily brought the real apple and handed it over to me, asked me to play with it to experience and tell me that was an apple. In fact, she did this for almost a week. See Figure P1.1.

The following week she brought a tomato and an apple and asked me to tell her which one was the apple. I was able to correctly point out the apple without any hesitation (Figure P1.2).

Now let us come to the point: what do you think the teacher has done to make the student recognize it so well? Yes, the teacher patiently *"trained"* the student with an original apple for a week and the features of the apple such as its red color, round shape and properties of being white and hard inside; all have been registered properly by experiencing it. This collective intelligence gathered by the student helped them to recognize the apple from a different fruit like tomato during a *"testing"* phase. (By the way, we are not providing false information: Tomatoes are fruits that are considered vegetables by nutritionists as suggested by Britannica.com.)

Figure P1.2 Teacher testing the student if they correctly recognize the apple.

So, let us discuss the question again: "What is machine learning?" How is it even relevant to the example given above? Now carefully answering this question, by the literal meaning of machine learning, we are trying to make a machine learn. Yes, we feed already known data to a machine and *train* it. Once the machine is trained appropriately, we will *test* the machine to see whether the machine is able to provide the apt answers with the help of the trained data. We can keep training the machine until it provides us the most optimized results.

Oh, that is all. Isn't it? Machine learning is all simple now and makes sense.

Figure P1.3 correctly depicts the machine learning process in a simple way. The machine takes a picture of an apple as an input, manually extracts the features of the apple and uses the information to learn. This is basically done by various machine-learning algorithms, which are available to create an ML trained model. This ML trained model is provided with test data to check whether the model predicts accurately or not. The major point to be noted here is that, in any machine learning process, the feature extraction is very important and would be done without human intervention.

P1.3 RELATIONSHIP BETWEEN AI, ML, AND DL

Artificial Intelligence (AI) is the broad area of research where researchers started thinking of inducing intelligence to machines. You may all know Sophia, the first humanoid robot who has citizenship of Saudi Arabia. Tang

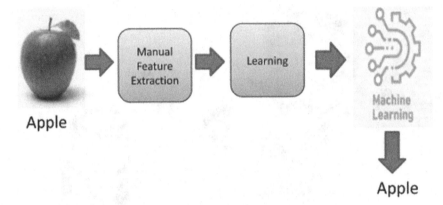

Figure P1.3 Machine learning process.

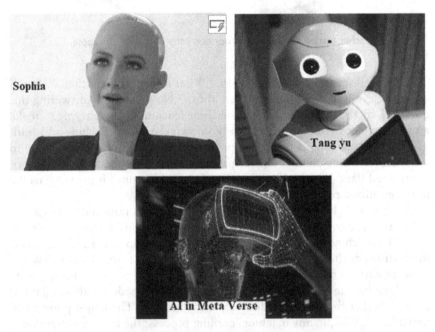

Figure P1.4 Humanoid Robot Sophia, Robert CEO Tang Yu and AI in Metaverse.

Yu is the AI-driven virtual robot CEO, who has been appointed to optimize the operational efficiency. The whole concept of AI in metaverse swirls around the fact that people do not need to face any real-life risks as they face in a real-life environment. See Figure P1.4.

In this epoch of AI, ML is a beautiful subset of AI, which allows a specific task to be performed without any explicit interventions. Data from the past is provided to the system; the system extract features and learns from the patterns identified. Certain inferences are made from patterns and accordingly intelligent decisions are taken. Machine learning algorithms are auto adaptive and hence no explicit human interventions are required for the learning process of models. Feature extraction is an important step in the whole process, which helps the model to predict or classify the data appropriately.

Deep learning (DL) is an advanced subset of AI, where a human brain is imitated in processing and understanding the data. Neural networks tend to be the basis of deep learning, which mainly acts like a black box to grab data and yield wonderful insights. Interpreting the results from the deep neural networks require good analytical skills so that the output obtained makes sense for some other useful applications.

Figure P1.5 shows a proper relationship between AI, ML, and DL. Some of the major applications of AI like Natural Language Processing (NLP), visual perception by visualization techniques, automated programming platforms like no code, AI-driven robots for strenuous jobs and household jobs, knowledge representation and reasoning are some of the major applications that comes under AI.

Machine learning has many algorithms like regression, classification, principal component analysis, clustering etc. for finding the inferences from the data analyzed using models created. Multilayer Perceptron's used in Neural networks with the help of various algorithms like CNN (Convolutional neural networks), RNN (Recurrent Neural Network), GAN (Generative Adversarial Networks), automatic feature extraction and prediction or classification could be achieved using deep learning. The evolution progress of various categories of algorithms is portrayed in Figure P1.6.

PI.4 TYPES OF MACHINE LEARNING

Now that we have a deep understanding about where machine learning has its place in the AI field of research, it is time for us to understand the various types of machine learning algorithms. Machine learning algorithms are mainly classified as three as given below; however, we add a fourth category for in depth understanding (see Figure P1.7).

- Supervised learning
- Unsupervised learning
- Reinforced learning
- Evolutionary learning

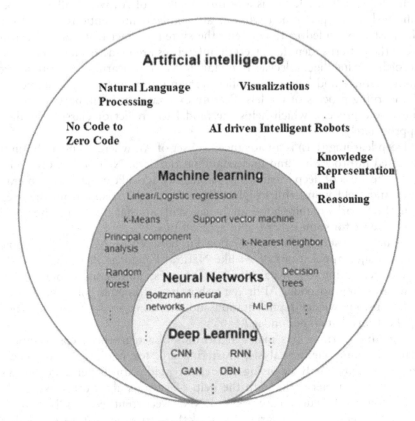

Figure P1.5 Relationship between AI, ML, DL.

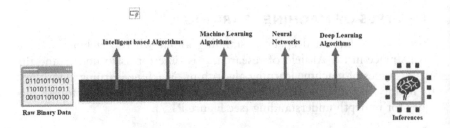

Figure P1.6 How each of the category of algorithms evolved over time.

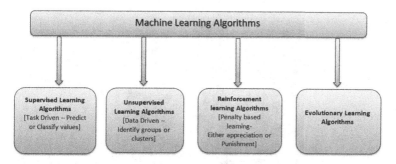

Figure P1.7 Types of machine learning algorithms.

Let's have a deeper look into the same with easy examples.

P1.5 SUPERVISED LEARNING ALGORITHMS

This algorithm makes use of labelled data gathered from the past to train the model and make the model predict or classify the test data which is not labelled to check whether the model can predict or classify the data properly. Supervised machine learning algorithms use labelled data – what is meant by that? It is simple – consider an example to understand the supervised learning process.

You are provided with a dataset that contains images of both cats and dogs (Figure P1.8). All the images in the dataset are labelled properly, say you have 1,000 images of both cats and dogs each. You are creating a supervised learning model where you train the model using 700 labelled cat data and 700 labelled dog data. You have kept 300 cat and dog images as test data (Figure P1.9). Once the supervised machine learning model is created, we will make the model predict these test data and check the accuracy of the model created.

As we now understand what is there in the datasets, we shall proceed with the process.

The complete supervised learning process is provided in Figure P1.10. In the supervised learning model, we work with labelled data, which is fed into the model for training, once the model is trained, test data is fed into the model to either classify or predict the test data. The accuracy of model prediction is usually calculated as an evaluation metric to understand the efficacy of the trained model.

One major point to be noted here is that, if the model is trained using wrong labelled data, of course the model will predict in a wrong manner. Hence the training data fed to the model need to be appropriately labelled ones. Another scenario might be, if the model is not trained with a certain

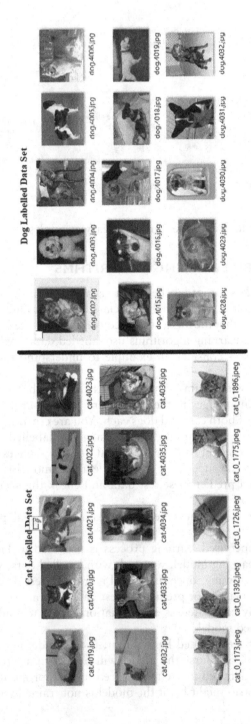

Figure P1.8 Sample – cat and dog labelled training data set.

cat_or_dog_1.jpg   cat_or_dog_2.jpg

Figure P1.9 Sample test dataset with name as cat_or _dog_1 and cat_or _dog_2.

labelled data and if an entirely new data is given for prediction, the percentage of accuracy will be extremely low. This is quite understandable. If you have cats and dogs in the dataset and is given for training the model, and if you give the test set as crocodile, there is a higher chance that the trained model might not be able to predict or wrongly predict the data.

The first Figure P1.1 of a teacher teaching a student about the apple is also an example of supervised learning. Maybe you should revisit that example once again to embed the concept well into your mind.

P1.6 UNSUPERVISED LEARNING ALGORITHM

This approach is different from the supervised learning model, as they don't have any labels associated with the data. Also, there is no explicit training and testing phases in the unsupervised learning method. Oh, is this not confusing? Then how will the model be able to predict. Yes, there is a way, and we could understand that by using athe simple example that follows.

Consider a student is given a dataset with set of dogs and cats, with absolutely no label (Figure P1.11). Every day this dataset is given to the student and after a week the student is asked to categorize the similar images in the dataset. What do you think the student will do? The student has been going through the different types of images given for a week. The student would have been smart enough to identify the features of both the cat and dog images. By the end of the week, if different set of images are given, obviously with the collective knowledge he has gathered through the process of mapping the features of dog and cat, the student will at least to some extent map or group the cat and dog images properly. Yes, there are some cutie dogs which resemble dogs, we can't help it though, and hence there may be some misclassifications too (Figure P1.11).

Given a set of data, it will categorize them and give as output. Each category is referred as a cluster. The labels for the clusters are to be manually tagged later. The categorization is based on the features in the data

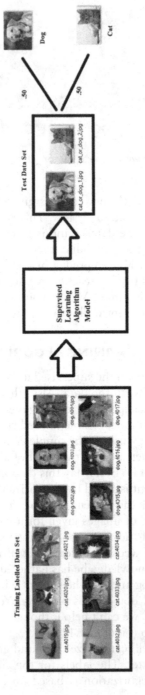

Figure P1.10 The complete supervised learning process.

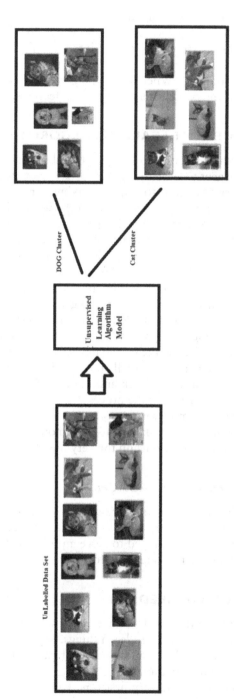

Figure P1.11 Unsupervised learning process.

points. The unsupervised learning algorithms are also referred as clustering algorithms. Consider the same use case discussed for supervised learning with apple and tomato. Here the model will take in all images and gives out two clusters. One cluster will be "apple" whereas another cluster will have all the photos of "tomato." When a new image is given to the model it will be placed in one of the two clusters based on its features.

P1.7 REINFORCEMENT LEARNING ALGORITHM

Reinforcement learning algorithm is a machine learning algorithm, which uses the computer agent to learn the optimal behavior of the environment and ought to take the right actions to acquire maximum reward. This is mainly about the decision-making process for which the feedback obtained is very crucial. This is a feedback-based learning process. This method of learning is used in most of the robots and computer-based games. Here the input need not have labelled data. Instead, the model learns by interacting with the environment and getting feedback from it. The first time the model picks a decision, based on the feedback the model learns if its decision is right or wrong. So, this supervised learning relaxes the task of giving completely labelled data for training. A very common example is a computer chess game; if the computer loses while playing with you, then the program will remember all the steps that the player made, and the system made. Next time, the same strategy won't work in the system and eventually the player will lose to the program.

Oh, does all this seem to be Greek and Latin? Don't worry, we'll use an example to help you understand the process.

Let's take a simple example for reinforcement learning. Consider a mom teaching her kid and when he makes mistake, mom gives feedback so that the feedback could be helpful for him the very next time (Figure P1.12).

P1.8 EVOLUTIONARY APPROACH

This is still evolving and is not an easy one. These types of algorithms shall imitate the natural evolution to solve a particular problem. For instance, genetic algorithms can be employed to solve a problem. This is beyond the scope of this book and hence is ignored for now.

P1.9 SO WHY DO WE NEED ML?

This is a wonderful question, at the right time. Yes, by this time, it is obvious that we use our own experience to learn things. Say, for a simple example, going back to childhood. Yes, childhood is a treasure full of experiences, right? So let's use another example...

Do you ever remember the very first time your hand got hurt touching a hot vessel in the kitchen? It's likely that unless it was a big one, no one

What's this my son?

Mom, it is an orange.

No, My boy, it is Apple.   This is the feedback!

Oh, Apologies mom, I shall correct

What's this my son?

Mom, it is an apple

Figure P1.12 Reinforcement learning.

usually even remembers that instance? However, now you are old, do you still need somebody's assistance to understand whether a vessel is hot, and when you shouldn't touch it? Here you could understand the experiential learning. Maybe when you were a kid, you would have touched a hot pot and instantly you would have got the impulse. That feedback stays in your collective memory and whenever you see a pot, you just take a precaution to work out whether it is hot or not.

Yes, we humans have the intelligence to do all these things. But we cannot reach everywhere and do this sort of things always. But we do have the intelligence to program a machine to follow our orders. This is exactly what we are trying to do in machine learning. Yes, so why do we do all these? The reason is this will make our lives easy. If we can build an interactive and self-adaptive learning algorithm for a machine and if we could train the machine in the way we need to achieve things, there is nothing like it. However, everything has its own flaws coming along. As humans, first, we should know where to limit the usage of machines and to what extent. Anything and everything could be trained for negative intention too.

Where humans cannot bring the accuracy, yes, machines could bring this. So, making the machines work using human intelligence is a good strategy. Machines with ML algorithms don't require explicit human intervention as mentioned earlier and machines can always adapt to their environments and learn from feedback and avoid repeated mistakes.

P1.10 MACHINE LEARNING FRAMEWORK

A Machine learning framework has various steps which uses math, tools, and techniques. The first step is all about data gathering from the alternative relevant sources. It all starts from data, as data acts as the fuel for the whole process. The next step is basically data cleansing or an extensive exploratory data analysis step where we need to clean and understand the data as much as possible, as this will help further processes to be smooth, easy, and inferential. Building the appropriate model is the next one in the process. Training and testing need to be done. The most important part is understanding the patterns from the results and interpreting the right inferences for the betterment of the whole process itself. Visualization techniques could be of great help to understand the hidden golden nuggets of information from the results. This concludes the flow of ML framework. However, as a picture can speak a thousand words, let's depict the whole process flow as a simple diagrammatic representation (Figure P1.13).

P1.11 MACHINE LEARNING VS. DEEP LEARNING

Yes, now we have been talking about the machine learning algorithms, its types, framework etc. Now it is time to dive a little bit deeper and understand the major differences between ML and DL algorithms. The difference in their process flow can be better understood from Figure P1.14 and Table P1.1 differentiates the two.

P1.12 ML COMMON APPLICATIONS

- Some of the common ML applications you have already experienced in your life:
- FB (Facebook) recommending you friends.
- Amazon recommending you products.
- Flipkart recommending you products.
- Netflix recommendations.
- Netflix recommending you the best series based on your taste but with ML behind. So, the point is simple. With ML in picture, a company can identify more opportunities for making good profits. A scenario – you are browsing Thailand holidays. You did not book any tickets or even confirm the trip. Upon logging in to your Facebook account, you

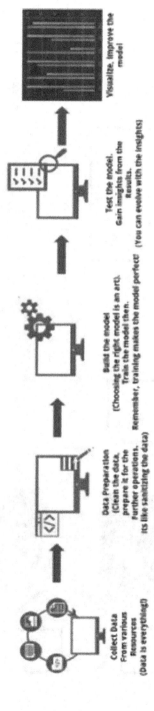

Figure P1.13 Machine Learning Framework.

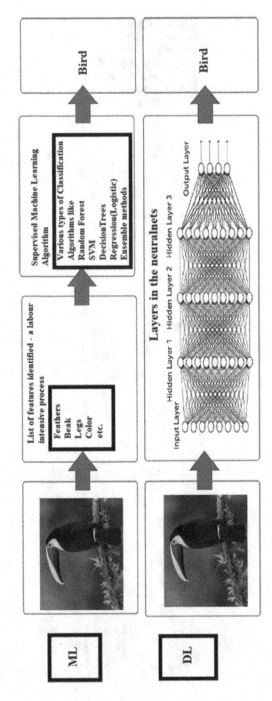

Figure P1.14 Difference in process flow with ML and DL.

Table PI.I ML vs. DL

Machine Learning	Deep Learning
Requires only less amount of training data	Requires large amount of training data
ML works on pre-identified features	DL automatically identifies the features
Results are easily interpretable	Interpreting the results needs some expertise
ML uses various algorithms to conclude	DL uses neural networks to conclude

will be getting Thailand holiday-related posts. This is ML for you! It helps in finding avenues for new business, enhancing profit all without any errors or human intervention. No operator is there to link that Thai AD (advertisement) to Facebook page yet.

- Another major application of ML is in:
- Agriculture sector – To identify crop diseases.
- Energy sector – to predict the consumption of energy for a region in the next two months.
- Education sector – predicting the number of students completing the course and the job openings in the market.
- Government sector – many ML-related applications are used, as an example automating and identifying the unique identification number from the captured image of a person for recognition purposes.
- Financial sector, media sector, retail sector, smart home and telecom are some of the other sectors where we frequently employ machine learning concepts.

Well, we have understood the fundamentals of machine learning and this book is intended to get the readers insights on how to build some cool machine learning projects. All these projects are easy to do and will definitely help in understanding ML concepts/algorithms clearly. The datasets, code, and clear explanations are provided to ensure that readers have a smooth learning experience.

Also, we have used the Intel oneAPI as a platform to implement some of the ML projects. With this approach, readers will get to know oneAPI, get the learning clearly about the Intel Developer Cloud, know optimized libraries and enhanced frameworks usage through oneAPI. It is important not just to program, but also to ensure that the code is written in an optimized manner.

The ensuing section is intended to get you the knowledge about oneAPI.

PI.I3 WHAT IS oneAPI?

What is oneAPI? Well, this is a question asked by many tech enthusiasts, learners, teachers, industry practitioners and everyone in the tech space. This chapter is intended to provide information as to what oneAPI is all about, why there is a lot of discussion about oneAPI, what oneAPI can provide, etc. (Note: It is oneAPI and not OneAPI.) Let us first understand the problem faced by software developers all around the world. Firstly, there has been humongous growth recently in specialized workloads. Secondly, each hardware needs to use different programming languages and related libraries. This increases the challenges with respect to maintaining different code bases and repositories. Thirdly, though it is seen as an advantage with the increase in the number of tools, it is also a challenge for developers to learn to use different tools, particularly given the learning time involved. What we mean here is that the development of software for different hardware platforms like CPU (Central Processing Unit), GPU (Graphics Processing Unit) or FPGA (Field-Programmable Gate Array) requires different learning strategies, investments and eventually no guarantee of reusing that work with other architectures/hardware. Writing code once, then writing it again for another architecture is the biggest bugbear faced by software developers globally. Yes, this problem has to be solved and this is where oneAPI comes in.

One can understand the aforementioned point by referring to Figure 1.15 which is self-explanatory. The challenge to be solved is huge and that is where oneAPI comes in handy.

One must first understand what oneAPI all is about. It is an open and standards-based cross architecture programming model which breaks the programmers' challenges. oneAPI provides the developers with total freedom and choice to select the hardware as CPU, GPU, or FPGA for enhanced computing. The vision behind the oneAPI's creation is interesting. It aims to bring a unified software development environment across CPU, GPU, or other accelerators.

oneAPI is an industry initiative and is completely based on the standards and the open specifications.

oneAPI has many appreciable features which developers certainly appreciate:

1. First and foremost, the developers can develop and deploy the software with absolute peace of mind.
2. oneAPI includes libraries and has a unified language which can ensure complete native performance.
3. Freedom, yes. oneAPI facilitates the native code performance across a range of hardware including CPUs, GPUs, FPGAs, and AI (Artificial Intelligence) accelerators.
4. Since it is of open industry standards, it is certainly the best approach for the future.
5. The biggest advantage lies with the compatibility. Yes, it gives you excellent compatibility with the existing programming languages which include the C++, Python, SYCL, Fortran, and openMP.

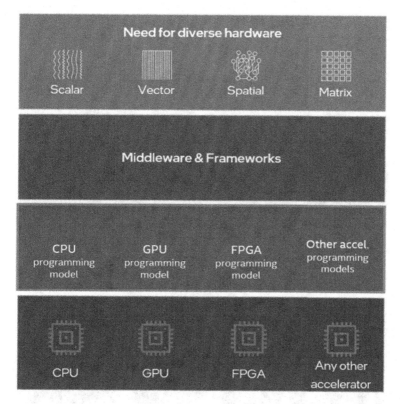

Figure P1.15 The challenge.

oneAPI is the foundational or base programming stack. Once should see that as a facilitator to optimize the middleware and the frameworks which gets above it. One can have a clearer understanding of this point by referring to Figure P1.16. The readers could see that TensorFlow kind of frameworks sit above the oneAPI which are optimized for performance. The representation shown in Figure P1.16 is enhanced and presented in Figure P1.17 to impart ample clarity.

The optimized applications go to the topmost layer as one could see from Figure P1.17, which leverages the middleware and the frameworks.

The oneAPI comes with powerful and advanced porting tools (this eases our job, folks, it ports the code for us). Analysis tools like the intel VTune profiler, intel advisor, and debuggers are also provided. This enables someone to debug the code or to analyze the performance across all levels of abstraction without any hindrance.

Having explained what oneAPI and what it brings to you as a developer, it is important to talk about another very important benefit it offers to the

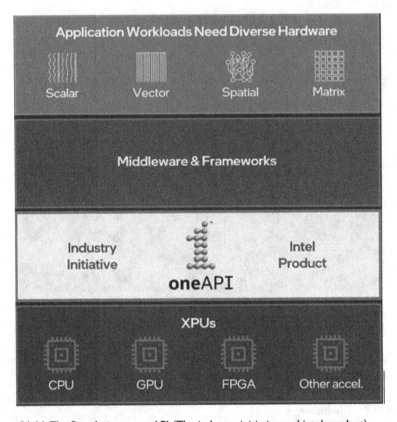

Figure PI.16 The Revolution – oneAPI (The industry initiative and intel product).

developers. There is no proprietary lock-in associated with oneAPI and is compatible with the code written in the native languages such as C, C++ and more as conveyed earlier.

In simple words, oneAPI provides developers the option to choose the best of the architecture for a specific problem without forcing the developer to re-write the code for different architectures or platforms.

oneAPI also promotes community and industry collaboration on a larger scale.

Remember this! oneAPI is all about "Write once, deploy many times."

PI.14 APPROACHES: DIRECT PROGRAMMING AND API BASED

oneAPI is interesting. There are two options provided to the developers for programming. One is direct programming, and the second option is

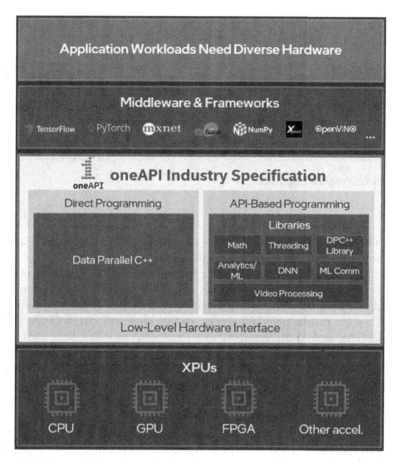

Figure P1.17 Power of oneAPI.

API-Based Programming. In addition, DPC++ provides the compatibility tool and the debug tools with oneAPI (Figure P1.18).

- The developers working with CUDA and who has the requirement to migrate the existing CUDA code (CUDA Source Code) to the DPC++ (DPC++ Source Code) is easier right now with oneAPI. oneAPI provides you the intel DPC++ Compatibility Tool to migrate source code to source code to from CUDA to DPC++ with ease. There is a lot of assistance offered in the migration and almost 80 to 90 percent automatically. The best part is "inline comments" are also provided in an understandable manner for the developers to finish the porting.

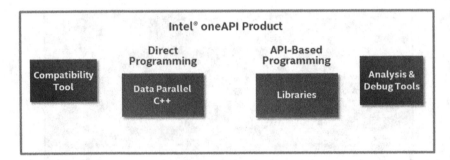

Figure P1.18 Programming model.

- The intel oneAPI DPC++ / C++ compiler is very powerful, and it supports the direct programming. This approach comes into place when the APIs are not available for the algorithms. The readers shall be presented with more details about the direct programming. For direct programming, Data Parallel C++ (or DPC++) is an evolution of C++ for productive data-centric coding that will target CPUs, GPUs FPGAs, and AI accelerators.
- The next approach is the API based programming. There is a huge set of libraries catering to different domains and areas. Details of the libraries is presented in the subsequent section. Developers can just go ahead and use them without any challenge. Readers can find a lot of information on the libraries shortly.
- Finally, in Figure P1.18 you can also see that we have the tools like intel VTune Profiler and Intel Advisor which can help in analyzing performance.

P1.15 LIBRARIES – MORE POWER TO YOU

oneAPI comes with rich set of libraries which enable acceleration of domain-specific functions. All the libraries as shown in Figure P1.19 are preoptimized to ensure maximum performance. One could see that the libraries cater to vast domain requirements. These libraries simplify programming by providing developers with APIs.

A brief note on each of these libraries is presented below.

✓ Intel oneAPI Math Kernel Library – one could use this library to have the highly optimized math routines in their applications being developed.

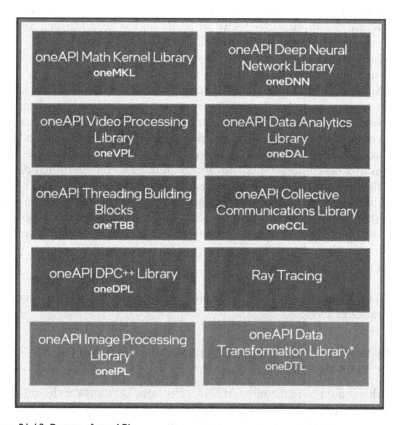

Figure P1.19 **Power of oneAPI.**

✓ Intel oneAPI Deep Neural Network Library – one could use this library to build the deep learning applications which uses the neural networks optimized for the intel hardware, be it processor or graphics.

✓ Intel oneAPI Video Processing Library – as the name indicates this library can be very handy to accelerate the video processing in the chosen application.

✓ Intel oneAPI Data Analytics Library – this is one of the best and industry needs this. One can use this library to have speed and performance in the big data applications.

✓ Intel oneAPI threading Building Blocks – often called TBB, this gives the developer a chance to combine the TBB-based parallelism on the Multicore CPUs and the SYCL device-accelerated parallelism in the chosen application.

✓ Intel oneAPI Collective Communications Library – this can be used where the applications focus primarily on the deep learning and the machine learning workloads.

✓ Intel oneAPI DPC++ Library – one can use this library for building high-performance parallel applications.

✓ Support in the form of Ray Tracing libraries – to build photorealistic visuals from studio animation to scientific and industrial visualizations.

✓ Intel oneAPI Image Processing Library – as the name implies, oneAPI contains image processing functionality, filters, geometric transformations, color and type conversions, and various 3D operations, that allows developers to take advantage of diverse computational devices through SYCL* APIs without changing their code(s).

✓ Intel oneAPI Data Transformation Library – this is a very innovative attempt from intel to provide ready-to-use, optimized data compression functions for diverse architectures. oneDTL is designed in such a way that, execution can happen on wide range of devices which include CPU, GPU etc.

In addition, Intel oneAPI has also a plethora of toolkits available offering a wide range of services.

P1.16 WHAT'S THE CONNECTION OF oneAPI WITH THIS BOOK?

Well, this should be in the mind of readers by now. Let's answer the question. Machine Learning (ML) concepts can be taught through various platforms and modes. We have chosen oneAPI. Machine Learning will be easier through this approach we believe. Also, it is the need for the hour in the industry. ML skills hand in hand with the oneAPI knowhow will be phenomenal. We are certain that the readers would enjoy this entire journey of learning.

P1.17 LEARNING RESOURCES

One of the greatest things Intel has done is to provide excellent learning resources for all levels. Be it novice to the expert, the materials and learning pathways provided are simply outstanding. Intel also provides case studies, reference codes through GIT, and more for the learners. Teachers have got the opportunity to become certified instructors for oneAPI and they get access to complete training materials, presentations, example codes, assignment questions and answers.

The below links can be used to learn more about oneAPI:

✓ Intro to oneAPI
https://intel.ly/3BBDmpr

✓ oneAPI Toolkits
  https://intel.ly/3fhSdOA
✓ Learning Paths
  https://intel.ly/3S9ErvV
✓ Community projects
  https://devmesh.intel.com/
✓ oneAPI DevCloud
  https://devcloud.intel.com/oneapi/

To become a certified instructor for oneAPI, one can go ahead and apply with the below link:
www.intel.com/content/www/us/en/secure/developer/oneapi/certified-instructor-apply.html
And remember, it is all free!

P1.18 THE INTEL DEVELOPER CLOUD – YOUR PATHWAY TO LEARNING!

The Intel Developer Cloud is interesting and a powerful sandbox which enables someone to develop, test and run the workloads across range of accelerators which include intel CPUs, GPUs, and FPGAs with the Intel oneAPI software stack. Not only this, but it also comes up with excellent tutorials, learning materials, codes for anyone to start using it comfortably.

Here is the process to register for the Intel Developer Cloud, for free.

1. Visit https://console.cloud.intel.com/. It will get you a page where you can find **Create an Account** option as shown in Figure P1.20.
2. It will prompt you to enter some basic details, which includes your name, email address, country of residence and password of your choice. It does not ask you for your credit card details and it is a great plus for the users. Once the details are filled in, click to verify your email (Figure P1.21).
3. There will be an email from intel with a verification code; thismust be filled in the column indicated. That's it, it is almost done (Figure P1.22).
4. After verifying, you will be prompted to select the tier option. Standard free option can be chosen if you do not plan to buy the access (Figure P1.23).
5. Once selected, it will take you to console home page as shown in Figure P1.24. Click on the training and workshops.
6. Once the training and workshops is clicked, it will get you to the training and workshops page and there will be a plethora of options as shown in Figure P1.25.

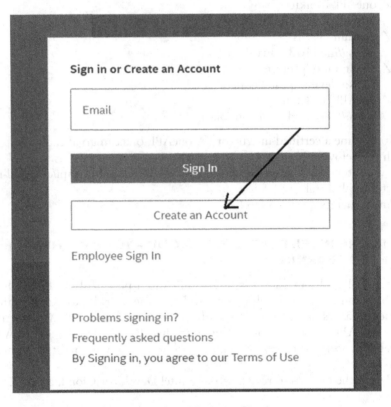

Figure P1.20 Create an account with Intel Developer Cloud.

7. On clicking machine learning using oneAPI, one can understand more details about the oneAPI and learning ML with oneAPI. Also, launch JupyterLab option under machine learning with oneAPI will get JupyterLab launched and one can try the ML experiments with oneAPI in this way (Figure P1.26).

8. The complete procedure is presented here: https://youtu.be/Mk_D jL3ZUVo

Welcome to the world of machine learning. Let's learn and create something wonderful.

RESOURCES

- Vasudevan, S.K., Pulari, S.R., & Vasudevan, S. (2021). Deep Learning: A Comprehensive Guide (1st ed.). Chapman and Hall/CRC. https://doi.org/10.1201/9781003185635

< Back

Please provide the following details.

Email	Confirm Email

First Name	Last Name

Language ⌄	Country/Region ⌄

New Password 🚫	Confirm New Password 🚫

☐ I would like to subscribe to stay connected to the latest Intel technologies and industry trends by email and telephone. I can unsubscribe at any time.

By submitting this form, you are confirming you are an adult 18 years or older and you agree to share your personal information with Intel. Intel's web sites and communications are subject to our Privacy Notice and Terms of Use.

Next: Verify your email

Figure P1.21 Account creation.

Figure P1.22 Account Verification.

Figure P1.23 Tier Selection.

- Murphy, Kevin P., 1970-, Machine Learning: A Probabilistic Perspective. Cambridge, MA, MIT Press, 2012.
- www.youtube.com/playlist?list=PL3uLubnzL2Tl-7fugIeCk4-14H VVdn5_v
- https://jupyter.org/
- www.intel.com/content/www/us/en/developer/tools/devcloud/overv iew.html
- Intel Developer Cloud – https://youtu.be/Mk_DjL3ZUVo

KEY POINTS TO REMEMBER

1. Machine learning is a branch of AI, which can help a machine learn and act imitating intelligent human behavior.

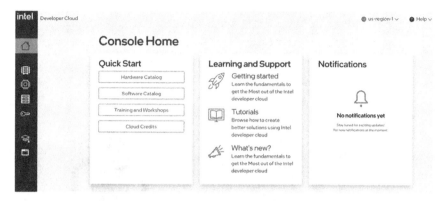

Figure P1.24 Cloud Console.

Training and Workshops

Launch JupyterLab

AI

AI Kit XGBoost Predictive Modeling
Learn predictive modeling with decision trees using Intel® AI Analytics Toolkit

Launch

Heterogeneous Programming Using Data Parallel Extension for Numba® for AI and HPC
Data Parallel Extension for Numba accelerates Python® code on Intel® XPUs

Launch

Machine Learning Using oneAPI
Intel® AI Analytics Toolkit accelerates data science and analytics with Python®

Launch

C++ SYCL

Essentials of SYCL
Learn to write performant and portable code using oneAPI and SYCL C++

Launch

Performance, Portability and Productivity
Learn to write performant and portable HPC code for multiple platforms with oneAPI and SYCL C++

Launch

Introduction to GPU Optimization
Learn GPU optimization techniques using SYCL.

Launch

Figure P1.25 Choose the training.

2. AI is the broader umbrella and machine learning and deep learning comes under them. All of them are related to each other.
3. Machine learning algorithms are categorized as supervised learning, unsupervised learning, and reinforcement learning. Evolutionary learning algorithms make use of genetic algorithms.
4. Supervised learning algorithms use labelled data set. They have a training phase to model and a testing phase to predict or classify the data. This is a classification problem.

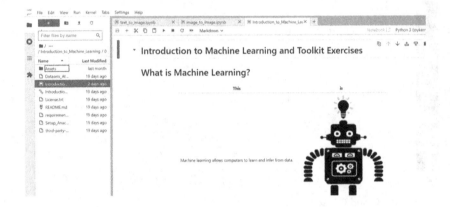

Figure P1.26 JupyterLab launch.

5. Unsupervised learning algorithms don't use labelled data; they categorize data into groups or clusters. This is a clustering algorithm.
6. Reinforcement learning gets feedback from the environment using computer agents and action and best utilize the parameters for optimal rewards.
7. Machine learning can perform adaptive learning, to bring in the best accuracy to the process, can take the feedback and make the process less error prone, and use them for recurrent tasks.
8. Machine learning framework mainly includes the following steps: data collection, data analysis, model building, testing the model, visualization, and results interpretation.
9. Machine learning uses ML algorithms to predict or classify the data whereas DL uses neural networks and its hidden layers to provide the output, which makes it a bit hard to understand and find the inferences.
10. Machine learning has many applications in various sectors like retail, agriculture, finance, healthcare, education, energy, government etc., apart from these FB recommending you friends, Amazon and Flipkart recommending you the products, Netflix movie recommendations etc.

## Chapter 1

Exploring the Iris dataset

LEARNING OBJECTIVES

By the end of this chapter, the reader should be able to:

- Obtain hands-on experience with machine learning (ML) techniques.
- Build an understanding of how to tackle comparable tasks and improve their knowledge of certain algorithms.
- Learn the essentials of working with a dataset, including how to load a dataset and examine its structure, as well as how to visualize the data patterns and relationships.
- Develop a strong basis in exploring ML projects and understand the benefits and drawbacks of various algorithms.

1.1 INTRODUCTION

In this chapter, we will set out on an adventure to investigate the Iris dataset and gain some understanding in the field of machine learning (ML). We will be able to classify Iris blooms using a variety of ML methods after doing analysis on this well-known dataset. This will allow us to understand the structure of the dataset, perform visualizations, and more.

The dataset is openly available in Kaggle datasets and readers can access it through this link: www.kaggle.com/datasets/uciml/iris

1.1 THE BEGINNING

To get started, let us proceed by loading the Iris data set as well as importing the required libraries.

In the code fragment snippet shown in Figure 1.1, the NumPy, Pandas, Seaborn, and Matplotlib libraries are imported. Additionally, we import the dataset Iris to a Pandas DataFrame titled "iris."

DOI: 10.1201/9781032676685-2

```
In [3]:  import numpy as np          # NumPy is a library for working with arrays of numerical data in Python
         import pandas as pd          # Pandas is a library for data manipulation and analysis
         import seaborn as sns        # Seaborn is a library for creating informative and attractive statistical graphics in Python
         import matplotlib.pyplot as plt   # Matplotlib is a library for creating static, animated, and interactive visualization
```

```
In [4]:  iris = pd.read_csv("Iris.csv")   # read the CSV file "Iris.csv" into a Pandas DataFrame called "iris"
```

Figure 1.1 Loading the dataset and importing the libraries.

```
In [5]:  iris.info()   # display information about the "iris" DataFrame, including the data types and number of non-null values fo
```

```
<class 'pandas.core.frame.DataFrame'>
RangeIndex: 150 entries, 0 to 149
Data columns (total 6 columns):
 #   Column        Non-Null Count  Dtype
---  ------        --------------  -----
 0   Id            150 non-null    int64
 1   SepalLengthCm 150 non-null    float64
 2   SepalWidthCm  150 non-null    float64
 3   PetalLengthCm 150 non-null    float64
 4   PetalWidthCm  150 non-null    float64
 5   Species       150 non-null    object
dtypes: float64(4), int64(1), object(1)
memory usage: 7.2+ KB
```

```
In [6]:  iris.head()   # display the first five rows of the "iris" DataFrame
```

Out[6]:

	Id	SepalLengthCm	SepalWidthCm	PetalLengthCm	PetalWidthCm	Species
0	1	5.1	3.5	1.4	0.2	Iris-setosa
1	2	4.9	3.0	1.4	0.2	Iris-setosa
2	3	4.7	3.2	1.3	0.2	Iris-setosa
3	4	4.6	3.1	1.5	0.2	Iris-setosa
4	5	5.0	3.6	1.4	0.2	Iris-setosa

Figure 1.2 Retrieving information from the dataset.

1.2 EXAMINING THE DATA

Let us investigate the structure of the Iris dataset in order to obtain some understanding of the data now that has been loaded.

We are able to retrieve information regarding the dataset by utilizing the *info()* method, including the data types and the amount of values that are not null contained within each column. With the *head()* method, we are able to investigate the initial five rows of the dataset (see Figure 1.2).

1.3 DATASET VISUALIZATION

When it comes to comprehending data patterns and relationships, visualizations are of critical importance. Let us make some visuals in order to obtain some understanding of the Iris dataset.

```
In [7]:  plt.boxplot([iris.SepalLengthCm, iris.SepalWidthCm, iris.PetalLengthCm, iris.PetalWidthCm],  # create a boxplot of the f
                labels=['SepalLength', 'SepalWidth', 'PetalLength', 'PetalWidth'])                    # label the boxplot with the na
         plt.show()  # display the boxplot
```

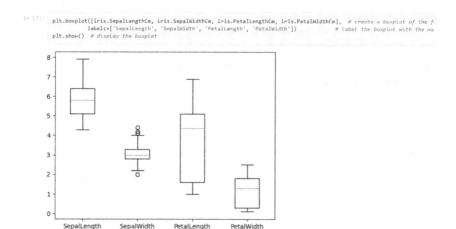

Figure 1.3 Boxplot visualization.

```
In [8]:  iris.Species.hist(edgecolor='red', linewidth=2);  # create a histogram of the "Species" column in the "iris" DataFrame w
```

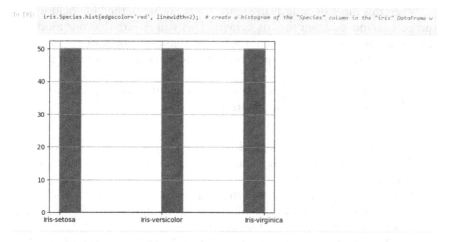

Figure 1.4 Histogram visualization.

The first type of representation is a boxplot, and it shows how the Sepal and Petal lengths of the flowers are distributed across the sample (Figure 1.3). It gives information about the range, median, and possible anomalies or outliers in the dataset. The second type of representation is a histogram, which illustrates the distribution of the different species of Iris (Figure 1.4).

We improve the histogram's overall aesthetic appeal by making it have red edges and setting the linewidth as 2.

1.4 CLASSIFICATION USING MACHINE LEARNING (ML) ALGORITHMS

Let us apply some machine learning techniques to the task of finding the iris flowers. We are going to apply three different algorithms: Logistic Regression (LR), Support Vector Machines (SVM), and Decision Trees.

You can use the following code to delete the column from the dataset if you want to remove the column yourself. We eliminate the "Id" column from the Iris dataset as it is not needed for the classification task.

The column in question is removed from the DataFrame by utilizing the *drop()* function, which can be seen in action in the following line of code. Providing it as the initial value causes the "Id" column to be removed from the result. When the *axis=1* parameter is used, it indicates that the action should be carried out in a column-wise fashion. In the end, the *inplace=True* parameter is provided to guarantee that the modifications will be reflected in the initial DataFrame (See Figure 1.5).

When this piece of code as in Figure 1.5 is executed, the "Id" field will be properly removed from the Iris dataset. This will ensure that our modeling and analysis tasks do not contain any superfluous information.

Use this code in order to import the essential machine learning components from scikit-learn.

The following packages and classes are brought in via import within this chunk of code as provided in Figure 1.6.

- *LogisticRegression* is derived from sklearn.linear_model and is a classification approach that is quite popular. This type offers functionality for logistic regression.
- *train_test_split* is a function that is derived from sklearn.model_selection. With the help of this function, we are able to divide the dataset into a training set and a testing set.
- *KNeighborsClassifier* is found in the sklearn.neighbors package. It is utilized by the k-nearest neighbors classification technique.
- *svm* module from sklearn supplies classification and regression techniques for use with support vector machines.

```
In [9]:  iris.drop('Id',axis=1,inplace=True) #dropping the Id column as it is unecessary, axis=1 specifies that it should be colu
```

Figure 1.5 Column removal.

```
In [10]:  from sklearn.linear_model import LogisticRegression  # import the LogisticRegression class from the sklearn.linear_model
          from sklearn.model_selection import train_test_split  # import the train_test_split function from the sklearn.model_sele
          from sklearn.neighbors import KNeighborsClassifier  # import the KNeighborsClassifier class from the sklearn.neighbors m
          from sklearn import svm  # import the svm module from sklearn
          from sklearn import metrics  # import the metrics module from sklearn
          from sklearn.tree import DecisionTreeClassifier  # import the DecisionTreeClassifier class from the sklearn.tree module
```

Figure 1.6 Code snippet to import ML components.

```
In [11]:  train, test = train_test_split(iris, test_size = 0.3)# in this our main data is split into train and test
          # the attribute test_size=0.3 splits the data into 70% and 30% ratio. train=70% and test=30%
          print(train.shape)
          print(test.shape)

          (105, 5)
          (45, 5)
```

Figure 1.7 Code snippet to divide the dataset.

- *metrics* is derived from the sklearn library. This module includes a variety of metrics for assessing the effectiveness of ML models.
- *DecisionTreeClassifier* is a popular classification approach based on decision trees. It comes from the sklearn.tree library.

Importing these modules and classes will provide you with access to the essential tools for creating and evaluating various ML algorithms on the Iris dataset. We will apply these algorithms to the dataset.

You may use the following piece of code (Figure 1.7) to divide the Iris dataset into training and testing sets by employing the *train_test_split* function provided by scikit-learn, and then report the shape of the sets that are produced as a result.

The iris DataFrame is to be partitioned into training and testing sets. The *test_size* parameter set to 0.3 indicates that 30 percent of the data is assigned to the testing set, while 70 percent of the data is for the training set.

After the data has been split, the form of the set used for training is printed utilizing the *shape* property of the *train* DataFrame, and then the testing set is printed utilizing the *shape* attribute of the *test* DataFrame. This is followed by printing the shape of the entire data set. This gives you the ability to check the lengths of the sets that are produced as a result.

When this code as in Figure 1.7 is executed, the Iris dataset will be partitioned into a training set and a testing set, with the corresponding shape of the sets displayed.

The training set's training features (*train_x*) along with training labels (*train_y*) are extracted here in this code block (see Figure 1.8). On the other hand, the testing features (*test_ x*) and testing labels (*test_y*) are taken from the testing set and extracted here. The characteristics are chosen in

```
In [12]: train_X = train[['SepallengthCm','SepalWidthCm','PetalLengthCm','PetalWidthCm']]# taking the training data features
         train_y=train.Species# output of our training data
         test_X= test[['SepallengthCm','SepalWidthCm','PetalLengthCm','PetalWidthCm']] # taking test data features
         test_y =test.Species  #output value of test data
```

Figure 1.8 Code snippet for extracting features.

accordance with the columns labeled "SepalLengthCm," "SepalWidthCm," "PetalLengthCm," and "PetalWidthCm," respectively.

A version of the Support Vector Machine (SVM) classification is built here using the *svm.SVC()* function. After that, the *fit()* method is called, and the model is trained by making use of the training data (*train_ x* and *train_y*). The *predict()* method is then used to make predictions based on the training model regarding the labels that should be assigned to the test features (*test_ x*). The correctness of the SVM model is determined with the *accuracy_ score()* function included in the *metrics* module to compare the labels that are predicted with the actual labels (*test_y*). The determined accuracy score is printed underneath (see Figure 1.9).

In a similar fashion, a version of the Logistic Regression (LR) classification is generated by calling the *LogisticRegression()* function. The model is then trained and evaluated in the same way to that of the previous SVM classification. In addition to that, the accurateness of the LR strategy is also printed (see Figure 1.10).

By following the code snippet as in Figure 1.11, a version of the Decision Tree classification called *DecisionTreeClassifier()* is generated. The model is then trained and assessed in the same manner to that of the previous two

```
In [13]:   model = svm.SVC() #select the algorithm
           model.fit(train_X,train_y) # we train the algorithm with the training data and the training output
           prediction=model.predict(test_X) #now we pass the testing data to the trained algorithm
           print('The accuracy of the SVM is:',metrics.accuracy_score(prediction,test_y))#now we check the accuracy of the algorithm
           #we pass the predicted output by the model and the actual output

The accuracy of the SVM is: 0.9777777777777777
```

Figure 1.9 Code snippet for SVM classification.

```
In [14]:   model = LogisticRegression() # create a new instance of the LogisticRegression class and store it in the variable "mode
           model.fit(train_X,train_y) # fit the model to the training data by calling the "fit()" method with the training data as
           prediction=model.predict(test_X) # use the fitted model to make predictions on the test data by calling the "predict()"
           print('The accuracy of the Logistic Regression is',metrics.accuracy_score(prediction,test_y)) # calculate and print the

The accuracy of the Logistic Regression is 0.9555555555555556
```

Figure 1.10 Code snippet for LR classification.

```
In [15]:   model=DecisionTreeClassifier() # create a new instance of the DecisionTreeClassifier class and store it in the variable
           model.fit(train_X,train_y) # fit the model to the training data by calling the "fit()" method with the training data as
           prediction=model.predict(test_X) # use the fitted model to make predictions on the test data by calling the "predict()"
           print('The accuracy of the Decision Tree is',metrics.accuracy_score(prediction,test_y)) # calculate and print the occur

The accuracy of the Decision Tree is 0.9333333333333333
```

Figure 1.11 Code snippet for Decision Tree classification.

```
[10] model_name = ['SVM','Logistic Regression','Decision Tree']  # create a list of model names
     accuracy = [97.7,95.5,93.3]  # create a list of accuracy scores for each model in the same order as the "model_name" list
```

Figure 1.12 Code snippet to create accuracy scores.

```
%matplotlib inline  # set the backend of matplotlib to render the plots in the Jupyter notebook
import warnings  # import the "warnings" module to ignore any warning messages
warnings.filterwarnings('ignore')  # ignore any warning messages that may be raised during the execution of the code
plt.figure(figsize=(10,5))  # create a new figure with a size of 10 inches by 5 inches
plt.title('Accuracy Comparison')  # set the title of the plot
plt.xlabel('Accuracy')  # set the x-axis label of the plot
plt.ylabel('Model')  # set the y-axis label of the plot
sns.barplot(x = accuracy, y = model_name)  # create a bar plot with the "accuracy" list as the x-axis values and the "model_name" list as the y-axis values
plt.tight_layout()  # adjust the layout of the plot to ensure all elements fit within the figure
plt.show()  # display the plot
```

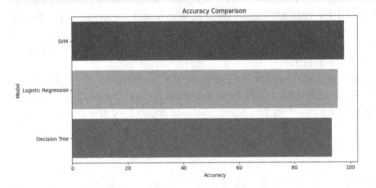

Figure 1.13 Code snippet to create accuracy scores and accuracy comparison.

models. The reliability of the Decision Tree concept is also displayed at the end.

Finally, the program generates a bar plot in order to contrast the degrees of accuracy achieved by each of the three models. The accuracy list stores the scores that match to the model names that are stored in the *model_name* list. The model's names are stored in the *accuracy* list (see Figure 1.12). The bar plot is produced by the *barplot()* function, which can be found within the seaborn library. The map produced as a result provides a visual representation of the accuracy of the comparisons between the chosen three models.

When the code as in Figure 1.13 is executed, it will show the accuracy values of the SVM, Logistic Regression, and Decision Tree models, in addition to the bar plot that compares the accuracy levels of the three models respectively.

1.5 INFERENCES

After carrying out an analysis of the accuracy levels of the chosen three models, we can infer that the SVM model obtains the highest level of accuracy, with Logistic Regression coming in a close second. In comparison to the other two models, the Decision Tree model offers a somewhat lower accuracy, however it is still reasonably accurate overall. We are able to make educated judgments about which approach is best suited for classifying Iris species of flowers based on the available attributes by contrasting and evaluating the accuracies of various models. This allows us to make informed choices about the paradigm that is ideally suited for classifying Iris flower species.

1.6 FUTURE LEARNING

With the information acquired in this chapter as a foundation, there are a number of fascinating avenues of research that can be pursued using the same or different datasets. The following are some potential areas that need to be taken into consideration: Advanced Feature Engineering methods to experiment with extra feature engineering techniques in order to boost the predictive capacity of the models. Investigate the domain-specific expertise you need to create new features, or think about altering the features you already have to gather additional relevant information from them. Investigation of several types of ensemble learning approaches, such as Random Forests, Gradient Boosting, or Stacking, can be done with the help of Ensemble Methods. Investigate how combining several classification models can increase the accuracy and resilience of the results.

SUGGESTED READINGS

Flake, G.W. and Lawrence, S., 2002. Efficient SVM regression training with SMO. *Machine learning*, 46, pp.271–290.

Friedrichs, F. and Igel, C., 2005. Evolutionary tuning of multiple SVM parameters. *Neurocomputing*, 64, pp.107–117.

Wang, Q.Q., Yu, S.C., Qi, X., Hu, Y.H., Zheng, W.J., Shi, J.X. and Yao, H.Y., 2019. Overview of logistic regression model analysis and application. *Zhonghua yu fang yi xue za zhi [Chinese Journal of Preventive Medicine]*, 53(9), pp.955–960.

Chapter 2

Heart failure prediction with oneAPI

LEARNING OBJECTIVES

By the end of this chapter, the reader should be able to:

- Explore the means of predicting heart failure by employing ML models and making use of the power provided by Intel's oneAPI framework.
- Use the oneDAL and oneDNN libraries that come along with the oneAPI.
- Obtain insights into predictive modeling and be in a position to apply those insights to comparable initiatives in the field of healthcare.
- Grasp the methods and algorithms that are used in the chapter.

2.1 INTRODUCTION

The process of investigating and analyzing data, developing models with a variety of methods, and evaluating the efficacy of these models in predicting heart failure will be covered in detail throughout this chapter. Building prediction models and gaining insights into this important area of healthcare will be accomplished with the help of a dataset on heart failure that is accessible to the general public. The link to the dataset is www.kaggle.com/datasets/andrewmvd/heart-failure-clinical-data

This chapter will improve both your theoretical understanding and practical competency in predictive modeling for heart failure prediction. You will have a better understanding of the significance of early diagnosis and precise prognosis in the process of bettering the outcomes for patients. In addition, you will gain an understanding of how to utilize well-known ML methods for heart failure prediction. The algorithms include random forest, XGBoost, and convolutional neural networks. You will also learn the benefits of leveraging Intel's oneAPI libraries, such as oneDAL and oneDNN, to optimize code, improve efficiency, and take advantage of hardware acceleration in order to boost performance.

DOI: 10.1201/9781032676685-3

Intel's oneAPI programming style and framework simplifies software development and optimizes performance across hardware architectures. oneAPI lets developers design code that runs efficiently on CPUs, GPUs, FPGAs, and other accelerators without major adjustments. This framework lets developers use hardware acceleration to accelerate computations with performance-optimized libraries like oneDAL and oneDNN. In this chapter, we optimize our code using oneAPI to improve the heart failure prediction models.

2.2 IMPORTING LIBRARIES

In this part, we import the libraries, which will be employed to work with data, analyze it, and build models that can predict what will happen. Each library has its own goal and gives us useful functions and classes to help us do our task.

- The pandas library gives us strong tools for manipulating and analyzing data, which makes it easy to work with structured data. The numpy library possess lot of math tools and makes it easy to do numerical calculations on arrays and matrices.
- We use the sklearn.model_selection module's train_test_split function to split the dataset into training and testing sets. This is very important for figuring out how well our models work on new data.
- We bring in the RandomForestClassifier class from the sklearn.ensemble package to build a random forest classifier model. Random forests are a type of ensemble learning that makes correct predictions by putting together several decision tree models.
- We add in the xgboost tool to do gradient boosting. Gradient boosting is used in XGBoost, which is a high-performance and efficient version of gradient boosting.
- In deep learning (DL), we use the tensorflow.keras.models package to bring in the Sequential class. With the Sequential class, we can make a neural network model with levels that are stacked on top of each other.
- Lastly, we bring in certain layers from the tensorflow.keras.layers package, such as Dense, Conv1D, MaxPooling1D, and Flatten. When making deep neural network architectures, these layers serve as the important building blocks.

Our code will be built on these imported packages, which will offer us the tools needed to analyze and model data well. The red bar below the code in Figure 2.1 depicts the optimization of oneDAL, oneDNN, and Xgboost libraries with oneAPI.

```
#Import the pandas library for data manipulation and analysis
import pandas as pd
#Import the numpy library for numerical computations
import numpy as np
#Import the train_test_split function from sklearn.model_selection module sed to split the dataset into training and testing sets
from sklearn.model_selection import train_test_split
#Import the RandomForestClassifier class from sklearn.ensemble module used for building a random forest classifier model
from sklearn.ensemble import RandomForestClassifier
#Import the xgboost library for gradient boosting
import xgboost as xgb
#Import the Sequential class from tensorflow.keras.models moduleUsed to create a sequential neural network model
from tensorflow.keras.models import Sequential
#Import the Dense, Conv1D, MaxPooling1D, and Flatten layers from tensorflow.keras.layers moduleUsed to add different layers to the neural network model
from tensorflow.keras.layers import Dense, Conv1D, MaxPooling1D, Flatten

2023-06-04 06:39:30.851523: I tensorflow/core/platform/cpu_feature_guard.cc:193] This TensorFlow binary is optimized with oneAPI Deep Neural Network Library (oneDNN) to use the following CPU instructions in performance-critical operations:  AVX2 AVX512F FMA
To enable them in other operations, rebuild TensorFlow with the appropriate compiler flags.
```

Figure 2.1 Importing the libraries.

2.3 EXPLORING THE DATA

In this section, we will go into the exploration of the heart failure dataset in order to obtain insights and better understand the data properties. The process of identifying patterns, links, and potential problems in a dataset is referred to as "data exploration," and it is a key stage in the ML pipeline.

We start by using the read_csv() function of the pandas library (see Figure 2.2) to load the heart failure dataset from a CSV file into a pandas DataFrame. Because of this, we are now able to efficiently organize and modify the data.

We use the head() function to display the first few rows of the dataset so as to get an overview of the data (see Figure 2.3). This clarifies the structure and format of the data for us, as well as the type of information that is stored in each column.

The next step is to acquire an overall perspective of the dataset by utilizing the info() function (see Figure 2.4). This gives us information on the data types that are contained within each column, as well as the total number of values that are not null. This is especially helpful in the identification of data that is either missing or incomplete.

Utilizing the describe() function allows us to generate a statistical summary, which provides us with further insights into the dataset. This summary provides measurements for each numerical column, such as the mean, standard deviation, minimum, maximum, and quartiles. It gives a detailed picture of the distribution of values within the dataset as well as the range of those values (see Figure 2.5).

```
#Read a CSV file 'heart_failure_clinical_records_dataset.csv' and store it in a pandas DataFrame named 'df'
df = pd.read_csv('heart_failure_clinical_records_dataset.csv')
```

Figure 2.2 Code snippet to read and store the dataset.

```
# Display the first few rows of the dataset
df.head()
```

	age	anaemia	creatinine_phosphokinase	diabetes	ejection_fraction	high_blood_pressure	platelets	serum_creatinine	serum_sodium	sex	smoking	time	DEATH_EVENT
0	75.0	0	582	0	20	1	265000.00	1.9	130	1	0	4	1
1	55.0	0	7861	0	38	0	263358.03	1.1	136	1	0	6	1
2	65.0	0	146	0	20	0	162000.00	1.3	129	1	1	7	1
3	50.0	1	111	0	20	0	210000.00	1.9	137	1	0	7	1
4	65.0	1	160	1	20	0	327000.00	2.7	116	0	0	8	1

Figure 2.3 To obtain data overview.

```
# Get an overview of the dataset including data types and non-null values
df.info()
```

```
<class 'pandas.core.frame.DataFrame'>
RangeIndex: 299 entries, 0 to 298
Data columns (total 13 columns):
 #   Column                    Non-Null Count  Dtype
---  ------                    --------------  -----
 0   age                       299 non-null    float64
 1   anaemia                   299 non-null    int64
 2   creatinine_phosphokinase  299 non-null    int64
 3   diabetes                  299 non-null    int64
 4   ejection_fraction         299 non-null    int64
 5   high_blood_pressure       299 non-null    int64
 6   platelets                 299 non-null    float64
 7   serum_creatinine          299 non-null    float64
 8   serum_sodium              299 non-null    int64
 9   sex                       299 non-null    int64
 10  smoking                   299 non-null    int64
 11  time                      299 non-null    int64
 12  DEATH_EVENT               299 non-null    int64
dtypes: float64(3), int64(10)
memory usage: 30.5 KB
```

Figure 2.4 To obtain data types.

```
# Compute statistical summary of the dataset
df.describe()
```

	age	anaemia	creatinine_phosphokinase	diabetes	ejection_fraction	high_blood_pressure	platelets	serum_creatinine	serum_sodium	sex	smoking	time	DEATH_EVENT
count	299.000000	299.000000	299.000000	299.000000	299.000000	299.000000	299.000000	299.000000	299.000000	299.000000	299.000000	299.000000	299.00000
mean	60.833893	0.431438	581.839465	0.418060	38.083612	0.351171	263358.029264	1.39388	136.625418	0.648829	0.32107	130.260870	0.32107
std	11.894809	0.496107	970.287881	0.494067	11.834841	0.478136	97804.236869	1.03451	4.412477	0.478136	0.46767	77.614208	0.46767
min	40.000000	0.000000	23.000000	0.000000	14.000000	0.000000	25100.000000	0.50000	113.000000	0.000000	0.00000	4.000000	0.00000
25%	51.000000	0.000000	116.500000	0.000000	30.000000	0.000000	212500.000000	0.90000	134.000000	0.000000	0.00000	73.000000	0.00000
50%	60.000000	0.000000	250.000000	0.000000	38.000000	0.000000	262000.000000	1.10000	137.000000	1.000000	0.00000	115.000000	0.00000
75%	70.000000	1.000000	582.000000	1.000000	45.000000	1.000000	303500.000000	1.40000	140.000000	1.000000	1.00000	203.000000	1.00000
max	95.000000	1.000000	7861.000000	1.000000	80.000000	1.000000	850000.000000	9.40000	148.000000	1.000000	1.00000	285.000000	1.00000

Figure 2.5 To generate a statistical summary.

2.3 MODELING PHASE

During the modeling phase, we incorporate optimization libraries into our workflow in order to improve the overall performance of the models. The oneDNN library is used in the optimization of the CNN model, whilst the oneDAL library is used in the optimization of the Random Forest model, both of which are performed within the context of the oneAPI framework.

In this section of code as in Figure 2.6, in order to separate the data, we make use of the train_test_split function that is available in the sklearn. model_selection module. We use the expression df.drop ('DEATH_EVENT',

```python
# Split the data into training and testing sets
X_train, X_test, y_train, y_test = train_test_split(df.drop('DEATH_EVENT', axis=1), df['DEATH_EVENT'], test_size=0.2, random_state=42)
```

Figure 2.6 Code snippet to divide the dataset.

axis=1) to represent the characteristics (X), and we use df ['DEATH_ EVENT] to represent the target variable (y). The test_size parameter, which determines the percentage of the data that will be allocated for testing, has its default value set to 0.2 (or 20%). The reproducibility of the split may be guaranteed thanks to the random_state argument.

After the data has been partitioned into the training set and the testing set, we are able to begin the process of instructing the models using the appropriate datasets.

2.3.1 Convolutional neural network (CNN)

To begin, we employ a convolutional neural network (CNN) in order to identify spatial correlations within the data. Convolutional layers, max pooling layers, and a dense layer are some of the components that make up the CNN model architecture. The CNN model is enhanced with the help of the oneDNN library; the red colored pop up in Figure 2.7 tells us that the Tensorflow binary is optimized with oneAPI Deep Neural Network Library. This library comes with DL calculations that is well optimized. It offers effective implementations of fundamental neural network operations such as convolution, pooling, and activation functions, among others. When the CNN model makes use of the oneDNN library, it is able to make use of calculations that have been optimized, which results in training and inference both being quicker and more efficient.

The model is compiled using the Adam optimizer and the binary cross entropy loss function, and we monitor the accuracy metric.

2.3.2 Random Forest classifier

Next, we begin the process of constructing a model by utilizing the Random Forest Classifier technique (see Figures 2.8 and 2.9). The Random Forest method of ensemble learning integrates the results of several different decision trees in order to produce predictions. The oneDAL library, also known as the oneAPI Data Analytics Library, is utilized in the process of optimizing the Random Forest model. This library is a component of the oneAPI framework. oneDAL is developed to speed up the processes of data analytics and provides optimized implementations of a number of different ML techniques, one of which being Random Forest.

2.3.3 XGBoost classifier

The final step that we do is to use the XGBoost Classifier, which is a streamlined version of the gradient-boosting algorithm. In a wide variety of machine learning applications, XGBoost has earned a reputation for its precision and performance (refer to Figure 2.10).

```
# Define CNN model architecture
model = Sequential()#Create a sequential model
#Add a convolutional layer with 64 filters, kernel size of 3 and ReLU activation function
model.add(Conv1D(filters=64, kernel_size=3, activation='relu', input_shape=(X_train.shape[1], 1)))
model.add(MaxPooling1D(pool_size=2))#Input shape is based on the number of columns in X_train and 1 channel
model.add(Flatten())#Flatten the output of the convolutional layer
model.add(Dense(1, activation='sigmoid'))#Add a dense layer with a single neuron and sigmoid activation function
#Compile the model with Adam optimizer and binary crossentropy loss function
model.compile(optimizer='adam', loss='binary_crossentropy', metrics=['accuracy'])
```

```
2023-04-13 21:27:48.686366: I tensorflow/core/platform/cpu_feature_guard.cc:193] This TensorFlow binary is optimized with oneAPI Deep Neural Network Li
brary (oneDNN) to use the following CPU instructions in performance-critical operations:  AVX2 AVX512F FMA
To enable them in other operations, rebuild TensorFlow with the appropriate compiler flags.
2023-04-13 21:27:48.777127: I tensorflow/core/common_runtime/process_util.cc:146] Creating new thread pool with default inter op setting:
```

Figure 2.7 Defining CNN model architecture.

```
# Train the model using training data
model.fit(X_train.values.reshape((-1, X_train.shape[1], 1)), y_train, epochs=10, batch_size=32, verbose=0)
```

```
<keras.callbacks.History at 0x7f311c972730>
```

Figure 2.8 Code snippet for training the model.

```
# Train the model using training data
model.fit(X_train.values.reshape((-1, X_train.shape[1], 1)), y_train, epochs=10, batch_size=32, verbose=0)

<keras.callbacks.History at 0x7f311c972730>

# Random Forest Classifier
from sklearnex import patch_sklearn
patch_sklearn()
rf = RandomForestClassifier(n_estimators=100, random_state=42)
rf.fit(X_train, y_train)

Intel(R) Extension for Scikit-learn* enabled (https://github.com/intel/scikit-learn-intelex)

    RandomForestClassifier
RandomForestClassifier(random_state=42)
```

Figure 2.9 Random Forest Classifier.

```
# XGBoost Classifier
from sklearnex import patch_sklearn
patch_sklearn()
xgb_clf = xgb.XGBClassifier(n_estimators=100, learning_rate=0.1, max_depth=3, random_state=42)
xgb_clf.fit(X_train, y_train)
```

```
Intel(R) Extension for Scikit-learn* enabled (https://github.com/intel/scikit-learn-intelex)
/glob/development-tools/versions/oneapi/2022.3.1/oneapi/intelpython/latest/lib/python3.9/site-packages/xgboost/sklearn.py:1146: UserWarning: The use of
label encoder in XGBClassifier is deprecated and will be removed in a future release. To remove this warning, do the following: 1) Pass option use_labe
l_encoder=False when constructing XGBClassifier object; and 2) Encode your labels (y) as integers starting with 0, i.e. 0, 1, 2, ..., [num_class - 1].
  warnings.warn(label_encoder_deprecation_msg, UserWarning)
[21:27:53] WARNING: /home/sat_bot/base/conda-bld/xgboost_1659485138838/work/src/learner.cc:1096: Starting in XGBoost 1.3.0, the default evaluation metr
ic used with the objective 'binary:logistic' was changed from 'error' to 'logloss'. Explicitly set eval_metric if you'd like to restore the old behavio
r.
```

```
▶   XGBClassifier

XGBClassifier(base_score=0.5, booster='gbtree', colsample_bylevel=1,
              colsample_bynode=1, colsample_bytree=1, gamma=0, gpu_id=-1,
              importance_type='gain', interaction_constraints='',
              learning_rate=0.1, max_delta_step=0, max_depth=3,
              min_child_weight=1, missing=nan, monotone_constraints='()',
              n_estimators=100, n_jobs=12, num_parallel_tree=1, random_state=42,
              reg_alpha=0, reg_lambda=1, scale_pos_weight=1, subsample=1,
              tree_method='exact', validate_parameters=1, verbosity=None)
```

Figure 2.10 XGBoost Classifier.

2.4 RESULTS AND DISCUSSION

We will evaluate the outcome of the trained models and conduct an analysis of the results received from the heart failure prediction task in this section. We will evaluate how accurate each model is, as well as compare the models' overall performance.

The correctness of each model is calculated and displayed using the code as in Figure 2.11. To determine how well the models can anticipate the incidence of heart failure, we use accuracy as a statistic to gauge how well they do so. When it comes to prediction, higher accuracy signifies better performance.

A bar plot can be used to visually represent the accuracy scores, which allows us to conduct additional research into the performance of the models and make direct comparisons between them (see Figure 2.12).

The accuracy ratings of the three models are presented in the form of a bar plot in Figure 2.12, which enables a speedy visual comparison of the respective levels of performance.

2.5 FUTURE LEARNING

While this chapter does provide some useful insights on predicting heart failure with the help of ML and Intel's oneAPI, there are still a number of potential areas where additional work and improvements might be made. The following are some probable regions that could be investigated in the future. Investigate any other features or data sources that could be able to supply more thorough information for the purpose of heart failure prediction. To improve the accuracy of the models' ability to predict outcomes, you might want to think about including genetic data, lifestyle factors, or other pertinent biomarkers. Techniques requiring advanced ML conduct research on more advanced ML algorithms and methods to see if these can produce better results for heart failure prediction. For instance, in order to capture temporal dependencies in patient data, one could use DL architectures such as recurrent neural networks (RNNs) or transformers. Model Optimization ensure the models are continuously optimized so that their precision and effectiveness can be increased. To determine which hyper parameter tuning strategies, model ensembles, or regularization methods produce the best results for each algorithm, you should do some experiments.

```
# Evaluate the models on the test set
cnn_score = model.evaluate(X_test.values.reshape((-1, X_test.shape[1], 1)), y_test, verbose=0)[1]
rf_score = rf.score(X_test, y_test)
xgb_score = xgb_clf.score(X_test, y_test)
```

```
# Print the test accuracy of each model
print('CNN Test Accuracy:', cnn_score)
print('Random Forest Test Accuracy:', rf_score)
print('XGBoost Test Accuracy:', xgb_score)
```

```
CNN Test Accuracy: 0.5833333134651184
Random Forest Test Accuracy: 0.75
XGBoost Test Accuracy: 0.7166666666666667
```

Figure 2.11 Model evaluation.

```
# Plot the accuracy of each model
import matplotlib.pyplot as plt
models = ['CNN', 'Random Forest', 'XGBoost']
accuracy = [cnn_score, rf_score, xgb_score]
plt.bar(models, accuracy)
plt.title('Model Test Accuracies')
plt.xlabel('Model')
plt.ylabel('Test Accuracy')
plt.ylim([0, 1])
plt.show()
```

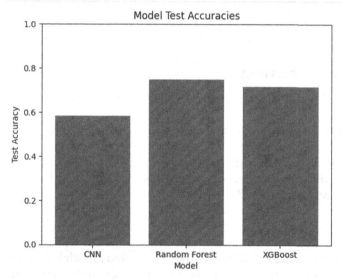

Figure 2.12 Plotting model accuracy.

SUGGESTED READINGS

Alzubaidi, L., Zhang, J., Humaidi, A.J., Al-Dujaili, A., Duan, Y., Al-Shamma, O., Santamaría, J., Fadhel, M.A., Al-Amidie, M. and Farhan, L., 2021. Review of deep learning: Concepts, CNN architectures, challenges, applications, future directions. *Journal of Big Data, 8,* pp.1–74.

Osman, A.I.A., Ahmed, A.N., Chow, M.F., Huang, Y.F. and El-Shafie, A., 2021. Extreme gradient boosting (Xgboost) model to predict the groundwater levels in Selangor Malaysia. *Ain Shams Engineering Journal, 12*(2), pp.1545–1556.

Sheridan, R.P., 2013. Using random forest to model the domain applicability of another random forest model. *Journal of Chemical Information and Modeling, 53*(11), pp.2837–2850.

Chapter 3

Handling water quality dataset

LEARNING OBJECTIVES

After completing this chapter, the reader shall be able to:

- Conduct an analysis of a water quality dataset in order to make accurate predictions regarding the potability of water.
- Acquire insights into the process of evaluating the safety of water by investigating the dataset, preprocess the data, deal with missing values, and construct ML models.

3.1 INTRODUCTION

The goals are to provide readers with the information and abilities necessary to work with datasets pertaining to water quality, comprehend the difficulty posed by class imbalance, and implement ML algorithms for predicting the potability of water. The readers can find the dataset in the following link: www.kaggle.com/datasets/adityakadiwal/water-potability

3.2 THE CLASS IMBALANCE PROBLEM

The problem of class imbalance is one of the challenges that frequently arises in the context of ML initiatives. Class imbalance is a circumstance in which the classes in the target variable are not uniformly distributed, with one class having a significantly lesser number of samples compared to the other class(es), as well as any further classes that might exist. This might happen in the context of evaluating the quality of the water when the number of water samples that are regarded to be acceptable for human consumption (class 1) is a significantly lower number than the number of samples that are considered to be harmful (class 0).

Dealing with class imbalance is crucial because it can lead to biased models that give priority to the class that holds the majority of the population and perform badly when it comes to accurately predicting the class that

DOI: 10.1201/9781032676685-4

holds the minority of the population. In order to guarantee accurate and trustworthy forecasts, we address the issue of class imbalance in the dataset pertaining to water quality in this chapter.

We use a pie chart to depict the distribution of the "Potability" classes in order to assess and overcome class imbalance. This helps us identify the imbalance between the safe and hazardous water samples, which is necessary for overcoming the problem. In order to solve this problem, it is ultimately decided to use resampling techniques. In order to achieve a dataset that is more evenly distributed, resampling may involve either oversampling the minority class (which would result in an increase in its representation) or under sampling the majority class (which would result in a reduction in its representation). We get rid of any possible biases that might have been caused by the order in which the data are presented by shuffling the dataset.

The reader will develop a better understanding of the class imbalance problem throughout the course of this chapter, as well as the significance of addressing it in an effective manner. Readers will learn how to generate a balanced dataset that provides equal representation of both safe and unsafe water samples by making use of resampling techniques. This will result in more accurate and dependable ML models for the prediction of water potability.

3.3 DATASET OVERVIEW

In this part, we import all the required libraries, read the data from the CSV file into a DataFrame, and show the first five rows of the dataset (see Figure 3.1).

3.3.1 Preprocessing the data

In this part, we deal with values that are absent in the dataset by adding the amount of missing data in every column and removing rows that have any missing values. The code snippet of the same is provided in Figure 3.2.

We use the isnull().sum() method to determine the amount of missing values in each column so that we can solve the issue of missing values in the dataset. This will provide us with a summary of the values that are missing from the dataset. We have decided to drop rows that include any missing values by using the dropna() method. This will allow us to ensure that the data is accurate and consistent. By carrying out these procedures, we have gotten an initial overview of the dataset pertaining to the water quality, which includes its structure as well as the way it deals with missing values. In the following sections, we are going to look deeper into the class imbalance problem that is present in the dataset and investigate different methods that can be used to overcome it.

In [1]:
```python
# import the pandas library for data manipulation and analysis
import pandas as pd

# import the NumPy library for numerical operations on arrays and matrices
import numpy as np

# import the 'train_test_split' function from the 'model_selection' module in scikit-learn
from sklearn.model_selection import train_test_split

# import the 'accuracy_score' function from the 'metrics' module in scikit-learn
from sklearn.metrics import accuracy_score

# read a CSV file and create a DataFrame
df = pd.read_csv("/content/water_potability.csv")

# display the first few rows of the DataFrame
df.head()
```

Out[1]:

	ph	Hardness	Solids	Chloramines	Sulfate	Conductivity	Organic_carbon	Trihalomethanes	Turbidity	Potability
0	NaN	204.890455	20791.318981	7.300212	368.516441	564.308654	10.379783	86.990970	2.963135	0
1	3.716080	129.422921	18630.057858	6.635246	NaN	592.885359	15.180013	56.329076	4.500656	0
2	8.099124	224.236259	19909.541732	9.275884	NaN	418.606213	16.868637	66.420093	3.055934	0
3	8.316766	214.373394	22018.417441	8.059332	356.886136	363.266516	18.436524	100.341674	4.628771	0
4	9.092223	181.101509	17978.986339	6.546600	310.135738	398.410813	11.558279	31.997993	4.075075	0

Figure 3.1 Importing the libraries.

```
# print the shape of the DataFrame
print(df.shape)

(3276, 10)

# count the number of missing values in each column
missing_values = df.isnull().sum()

# drop all rows that contain any missing values
df = df.dropna()
```

Figure 3.2 Solving the missing values in the dataset.

3.3.2 Class imbalance and oversampling

In this section, we will discuss the problem of class imbalance found in the dataset pertaining to water quality. When the classes in the target variable do not correspond equally to one another, it is known as class imbalance. In this instance, the "Potability" factor has classes that are not balanced, with one class having a substantially lower number of samples than the other class. We are going to make a pie chart to illustrate the distribution of the "Potability" classes so as to have a better idea of the class imbalance. This will assist us in gaining a better understanding of the distribution of each class within the dataset. The distribution of the students in the class can be seen in more detail using the pie chart as depicted in Figure 3.3.

We are able to view the percentage of each class, where "0" indicates water samples that are not suitable for human consumption and "1" indicates the water samples suitable for human consumption (see Figure 3.4).

We can see that there is a disparity between the classes using this graph. We take a larger sample size from the minority group so that we can address this issue utilizing resampling methods (see Figure 3.5). This helps to guarantee that the classes are more evenly distributed for model training. Last but not least; we shuffle up the dataset to eliminate any specific sequence biases.

From the pie chart shown in Figure 3.6, it is evident that after resampling we have solved the class imbalance problem.

3.3.3 Exploratory data analysis

We generate a heatmap of the correlation matrix by utilizing seaborn to acquire new insights into the links that exist between the variables (see Figure 3.7).

```
#Plots
import matplotlib.pyplot as plt
import seaborn as sns

# create a pie chart to visualize the distribution of Potability
df.Potability.value_counts().plot(kind='pie')
```

```
<Axes: ylabel='Potability'>
```

```
df.Potability.value_counts()
```

```
0    1200
1     811
Name: Potability, dtype: int64
```

Figure 3.3 Pie chart visualization.

```
zero = df[df['Potability']==0]   #zero values in Potability column
one = df[df['Potability']==1]  # one values in Potability column
```

Figure 3.4 To view the percentage of each class.

The heatmap that is produced as a result enables us to find relationships between various water quality characteristics. By conducting an analysis of the correlation values, we can gain a deeper comprehension of the dynamic relationship that exists between the variables and the potential influence that these variables have on the potability of the water.

3.3.4 Data splitting and model training

Next, we employ the train_test_split function that is part of the scikit-learn package to divide the dataset into a training set and a testing set. In addition

```
from sklearn.utils import resample
#minority class that is 1, we need to upsample/increase that class so that there is no bias
df_minority_upsampled = resample(one, replace = True, n_samples = 1200)
#concatenate
df = pd.concat([zero, df_minority_upsampled])

from sklearn.utils import shuffle
df = shuffle(df) # shuffling so that there is particular sequence
```

Figure 3.5 Code snippet to utilize resampling methods.

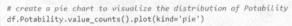

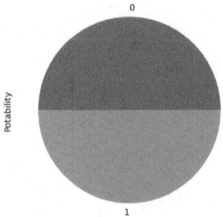

Figure 3.6 Pie chart visualization after resampling.

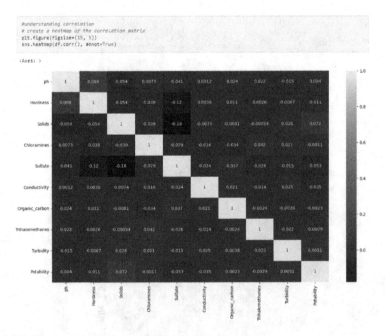

Figure 3.7 Generating a heatmap of the correlation matrix.

```
# create the feature set X and the target variable set y
X = df.drop('Potability', axis=1)
y = df['Potability']
# split the data into training and testing sets
X_train, X_test, y_train, y_test = train_test_split(X, y, test_size=0.2, random_state=42)
```

Figure 3.8 Splitting the dataset.

```
# import the LogisticRegression model from scikit-learn
from sklearn.linear_model import LogisticRegression

# create a new instance of the LogisticRegression model
model = LogisticRegression()

# train the model on the training data
model.fit(X_train, y_train)

# calculate the accuracy of the trained model on the testing data
lr = model.score(X_test, y_test) * 100

# print the accuracy of the LogisticRegression model on the testing data
print("Accuracy:", lr)

Accuracy: 86.458333333333336
```

Figure 3.9 Employing Logistic Regression algorithm.

to this, we import the necessary models for ML as shown in the code snippet of Figure 3.8.

Next, we are going to proceed with the process of training and evaluating three distinct ML models, namely Logistic Regression, Gaussian Naive Bayes, and Decision Tree Classifier.

3.4 LOGISTIC REGRESSION

The Logistic Regression algorithm is a common choice for use in binary classification projects. First, a new instance of the Logistic Regression model is created, and then it is trained using the provided training data. After that, we determine the trained model's performance on the testing data by computing its accuracy (see Figure 3.9).

3.5 GAUSSIAN NAIVE BAYES

A probabilistic approach frequently utilized for classification work is the Gaussian Naive Bayes. First, a fresh instance of the GaussianNB model is constructed, and then it is educated using the training data. After that, we

```
# import the Gaussian Naive Bayes model from scikit-learn
from sklearn.naive_bayes import GaussianNB

# create a new instance of the Gaussian Naive Bayes model
classifire = GaussianNB()

# train the model on the training data
classifire.fit(X_train, y_train)

# calculate the accuracy of the trained model on the testing data
nb = classifire.score(X_test, y_test) * 100

# print the accuracy of the Gaussian Naive Bayes model on the testing data
print("Accuracy:", nb)


Accuracy: 60.83333333333333
```

Figure 3.10 Employing Gaussian Naive Bayes algorithm.

compute the trained model's performance on the testing data and see how accurate it is (see Figure 3.10).

3.6 DECISION TREE CLASSIFIER

The Decision Tree Classifier is a flexible method that can handle classification as well as regression work. It is named after the decision tree that it is based on. We start by generating a fresh instance of the Decision Tree Classifier model, and then we train it using the provided training data. After that, we determine the accuracy of the trained model based on the testing data by using the following code as provided in Figure 3.11. The model comparison is presented in Figure 3.12.

```
# import the DecisionTreeClassifier model from scikit-learn
from sklearn.tree import DecisionTreeClassifier
# create a new instance of the DecisionTreeClassifier model
modelDT = DecisionTreeClassifier()
# train the model on the training data
modelDT.fit(X_train, y_train)
# calculate the accuracy of the trained model on the testing data
dt = modelDT.score(X_test, y_test) * 100
# print the accuracy of the DecisionTreeClassifier model on the testing data
print("Accuracy:", dt)


Accuracy: 80.83333333333333
```

Figure 3.11 Employing Decision Tree Classifier algorithm.

```
# import the required libraries
import matplotlib.pyplot as plt
# create lists of the model names and their respective accuracies
X = ["Logistic", "GaussianNB", "DecisionTree"]
Y = [lr, nb, dt]
# create a bar plot to compare the accuracies of the different models
plt.bar(X, Y, width=0.3)
# set the x-axis label
plt.xlabel("Model")
# set the y-axis label
plt.ylabel("Accuracy")
# display the plot
plt.show()
```

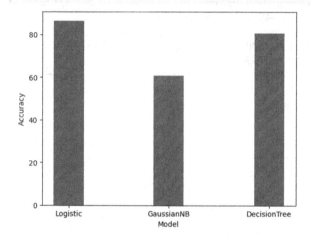

Figure 3.12 Model comparison.

3.7 COMPARISON OF MODELS

We use the matplotlib library to build a bar plot to evaluate and contrast the accuracy of the various models. We can establish which model performs the best in predicting the potability of water based on the accuracy scores.

We have determined that the Logistic Regression model performs the best in predicting the potability of water with an accuracy of approximately 86.45 percent.

3.8 FURTHER LEARNING

We have used machine learning to predict the water potability. We pre-process and handle the missing values first. Exploratory data analysis reveals feature connections in the water quality. We then employ Logistic Regression, Gaussian Naive Bayes, and Decision Tree Classifier models using training and testing sets and the best model is found by comparing their accuracy. This study delivers water quality forecast information that can improve community water safety decision-making.

Explore additional machine learning algorithms, optimize the model, or collect more diverse and comprehensive water quality datasets to further improve the water potability forecast accuracy and dependability.

SUGGESTED READINGS

Bi, Z.J., Han, Y.Q., Huang, C.Q. and Wang, M., 2019, July. Gaussian naive Bayesian data classification model based on clustering algorithm. In *2019 International Conference on Modeling, Analysis, Simulation Technologies and Applications (MASTA 2019)* (pp. 396–400). Atlantis Press.

Dayton, C.M., 1992. Logistic regression analysis. *Stat*, 474, p.574.

Japkowicz, N. and Stephen, S., 2002. The class imbalance problem: A systematic study. *Intelligent Data Analysis*, 6(5), pp.429–449.

Priyam, A., Abhijeeta, G.R., Rathee, A. and Srivastava, S., 2013. Comparative analysis of decision tree classification algorithms. *International Journal of Current Engineering and Technology*, 3(2), pp.334–337.

Chapter 4

Breast cancer classification with hybrid ML models

LEARNING OBJECTIVES

After finishing this chapter, the reader shall be able to:

- Make a prediction if the given sample in a dataset is benign or malignant.
- Utilize few well-known ML algorithms in the construction of hybrid models.
- Integrate several algorithms for improved predictive modeling.

4.1 INTRODUCTION

In this chapter, we will investigate the idea behind hybrid ML models. Kaggle has provided us with the Wisconsin Breast Cancer Dataset, which we will be using in our work. The purpose of this dataset is to make a prediction as to whether a given sample is benign (meaning it is not cancerous) or malignant (meaning it is cancer). Hybrid models are models that integrate different machine learning algorithms in order to capitalize on the characteristics of each individual method, which may result in enhanced performance and accuracy. k-Nearest Neighbors (k-NN), Support Vector Machine (SVM), and Random Forest are three well-known algorithms that will be utilized in the construction of hybrid models that we will focus on. You will have an understanding of the principles of hybrid machine learning models by the time you reach the conclusion of this chapter, as well as how to integrate several algorithms for improved predictive modeling. Readers can find the dataset in the following link: www.kaggle.com/datasets/uciml/breast-cancer-wisconsin-data

DOI: 10.1201/9781032676685-5

4.2 DATA PREPARATION

4.2.1 Importing libraries and loading data

To get things rolling, we need to begin by importing the required libraries for our work. We will be handling the data with pandas, performing numerical computations with numpy, and developing machine learning models with scikit-learn.

Afterwards, utilizing the read_csv() function as in Figure 4.1, we will import the data that is included within a CSV file to the pandas DataFrame. See Figure 4.2.

4.2.2 Exploratory data analysis

It is essential to carry out some preliminary examination of the data before beginning the modeling process. In order to comprehend and understand the data and its structure, we can make use of a variety of pandas functions. For instance, the head() function as provided in the code snippet of Figure 4.3 will show us the first five rows of the DataFrame; we may use head(10) to see the first 10 rows from the dataframe according to our convenience.

In order to deal with values which are not available in the dataset, we use the method isnull().sum() to search for any instances of null values. This gives the total amount of missing values that are present across all the columns in the DataFrame. To prevent biased or inaccurate predictions from being made, it is essential to manage missing data in an appropriate manner before training the models. See Figure 4.4.

Next, we split the data into features (X) and the target variable (y) using the train_test_split() function from scikit-learn. The "X" DataFrame contains the features used for prediction, while the "y" Series contains the corresponding target values. We split the data into training and testing sets, with 80% for training and 20% for testing. The random state parameter ensures reproducibility of the split. See Figure 4.5.

After we have split the data, the target variable will need to have its categorical values converted to numerical values (Figure 4.6). We replace the values of "y" variable by using the LabelEncoder method from the scikit-learn library (Figure 4.7). The letter "M" (for people who are affected by the disease = malignant) is substituted with 1, while the letter "B" (for people who are not affected by the disease = benign) is substituted with 0. In addition, we make use of the astype() method to change the data type of the "y" variable to an integer.

4.3 SCALING THE FEATURES

It is possible that various machine-learning algorithms will have varying requirements for the magnitude of the features. In this step, we will scale

```
# The read_csv() function from pandas is used to read the data from a CSV file named 'data.csv' and create a pandas DataFrame object named 'df'. This function can read CSV files from a local file system or from a URL.
# Once the data is read, it can be manipulated using pandas' built-in functions and methods.
df = pd.read_csv('data.csv')
```

Figure 4.1 Utilizing the read_csv() function.

```
import numpy as np                # Numpy is a library for working with arrays of numerical data in Python. We import it as 'np'.
import pandas as pd               # Pandas is a library for data manipulation and analysis in Python. We import it as 'pd'.
import matplotlib.pyplot as plt # Matplotlib is a library for creating visualizations in Python. We import the pyplot module as 'plt'.
from sklearn.model_selection import train_test_split   # The train_test_split function from scikit-learn is used to split data into training and testing sets.
from sklearn.preprocessing import StandardScaler   # The StandardScaler class from scikit-learn is used to standardize feature data.
from sklearn.ensemble import RandomForestClassifier   # The RandomForestClassifier class from scikit-learn is used to perform random forest classification.
from sklearn.svm import SVC       # The SVC class from scikit-learn is used to perform Support Vector Machine classification.
from sklearn.neighbors import KNeighborsClassifier   # The KNeighborsClassifier class from scikit-learn is used to perform k-nearest neighbors classification.
from sklearn.ensemble import VotingClassifier   # The VotingClassifier class from scikit-learn is used to perform ensemble classification by combining the predictions of multiple classifiers.
```

Figure 4.2 Importing the data.

```
# The head() method of a pandas DataFrame object is used to display the first 5 rows of the DataFrame.
# It is useful for quickly inspecting the data to ensure that it has been read in correctly and that the column headers and data types are as expected. By default,
# the head() method displays the first 5 rows, but you can pass a number n to the method to display the first n rows.
df.head()
```

	id	diagnosis	radius_mean	texture_mean	perimeter_mean	area_mean	smoothness_mean	compactness_mean	concavity_mean	concave points_mean	...	texture_worst	perimeter_worst	area_worst	smoothness_worst	compactness_worst	concavit
0	842302	M	17.99	10.38	122.80	1001.0	0.11840	0.27760	0.3001	0.14710	...	17.33	184.60	2019.0	0.1622	0.6656
1	842517	M	20.57	17.77	132.90	1326.0	0.08474	0.07864	0.0869	0.07017	...	23.41	158.80	1956.0	0.1238	0.1866
2	84300903	M	19.69	21.25	130.00	1203.0	0.10960	0.15990	0.1974	0.12790	...	25.53	152.50	1709.0	0.1444	0.4245
3	84348301	M	11.42	20.38	77.58	386.1	0.14250	0.28390	0.2414	0.10520	...	26.50	98.87	567.7	0.2098	0.8663
4	84358402	M	20.29	14.34	135.10	1297.0	0.10030	0.13280	0.1980	0.10430	...	16.67	152.20	1575.0	0.1374	0.2050

5 rows × 33 columns

Figure 4.3 Illustration of pandas function.

```
# The isnull() method of a pandas DataFrame object is used to identify missing or null values in the DataFrame.
# When this method is called on a DataFrame, it returns a DataFrame of the same shape as the original DataFrame, but with boolean values indicating whether each element is missing (True) or not missing (False).
#The sum() method is then called on this resulting DataFrame, which returns the total number of missing values for each column in the original DataFrame 'df'.
#This can be useful for identifying and handling missing data before performing any analysis or modeling.
df.isnull().sum()

diagnosis                  0
radius_mean                0
texture_mean               0
perimeter_mean             0
area_mean                  0
smoothness_mean            0
compactness_mean           0
concavity_mean             0
concave points_mean        0
symmetry_mean              0
fractal_dimension_mean     0
radius_se                  0
texture_se                 0
perimeter_se               0
area_se                    0
smoothness_se              0
compactness_se             0
concavity_se               0
concave points_se          0
symmetry_se                0
fractal_dimension_se       0
radius_worst               0
texture_worst              0
perimeter_worst            0
area_worst                 0
smoothness_worst           0
compactness_worst          0
concavity_worst            0
concave points_worst       0
symmetry_worst             0
fractal_dimension_worst    0
dtype: int64
```

Figure 4.4 To manage the missing data.

```
# assigns a new DataFrame 'X' to the result of dropping the 'diagnosis' column from the original DataFrame 'df'.
#The 'axis' parameter is set to 1, which means that the drop operation is performed on columns.
#This is done because 'diagnosis' is the target variable that we want to predict and it should be separated from the other features used for prediction.
X = df.drop('diagnosis', axis=1)
# assigns a new Series 'y' to the 'diagnosis' column of the original DataFrame 'df'. This will be used as the target variable for training and testing the machine learning models.
y = df['diagnosis']
# uses the train_test_split() function from scikit-learn to split the data into training and testing sets.
#The 'X' and 'y' data are split into 'X_train', 'X_test', 'y_train', and 'y_test', with a test size of 0.2 and a random state of 42. This means that 20% of the data will be used for testing.
#the random state ensures that the data is split in a reproducible way.
X_train, X_test, y_train, y_test = train_test_split(X, y, test_size=0.2, random_state=42)
```

Figure 4.5 Splitting the data.

```
# The first two lines of code are used to convert the target variable 'y' from categorical to numerical values.
# In this case, 'M' (indicating malignant) is replaced with 1 and 'B' (indicating benign) is replaced with 0.
#This is necessary because most machine learning algorithms cannot handle categorical data directly, and require numerical values instead.
y[y == 'M'] = 1
y[y == 'B'] = 0
# code uses the astype() method of a pandas Series object to convert the data type of the 'y' variable from object (i.e. string) to integer.
# This is necessary because most machine learning algorithms require the target variable to be of numeric data type.
y = y.astype(int)

<ipython-input-8-b5e81590157b>:1: SettingWithCopyWarning:
A value is trying to be set on a copy of a slice from a DataFrame

See the caveats in the documentation: https://pandas.pydata.org/pandas-docs/stable/user_guide/indexing.html#returning-a-view-versus-a-copy
  y[y == 'M'] = 1
<ipython-input-8-b5e81590157b>:2: SettingWithCopyWarning:
A value is trying to be set on a copy of a slice from a DataFrame

See the caveats in the documentation: https://pandas.pydata.org/pandas-docs/stable/user_guide/indexing.html#returning-a-view-versus-a-copy
  y[y == 'B'] = 0
```

Figure 4.6 Numerical values conversion.

```
from sklearn.preprocessing import LabelEncoder # imports the LabelEncoder class from the scikit-learn preprocessing module.
le = LabelEncoder()# creates an instance of the LabelEncoder class and assigns it to the variable 'le'.
# fit.transform() method of the LabelEncoder is used object to encode the target variable 'y'.
#The fit_transform() method first fits the encoder to the target variable 'y', which means it learns the mapping between the unique values in 'y' and their corresponding integer labels.
#Then, it applies this mapping to transform 'y' into an array of integer labels. The resulting encoded variable 'y' can be used as input to a machine learning model.
y = le.fit_transform(y)
```

Figure 4.7 Using LabelEncoder method.

the features so that they have an average value of zero and a variance of one using the StandardScaler tool that is part of scikit-learn (Figure 4.8). We use the StandardScaler class included in scikit-learn to normalize the feature data so that we can conduct fair comparisons and prevent some characteristics from being very influential in the models. We start by fitting the scaler to the training data, and then we use the learned scaling factors to change both the training data and the testing data.

4.4 BUILDING HYBRID ML MODELS

In this chapter, we will construct distinct ML models by utilizing the methods known as Random Forest, Support Vector Machine (SVM), and k-Nearest Neighbors (k-NN). The aforementioned models will act as the foundation for our hybrid model, which will be based on them.

4.4.1 Random Forest + SVM model

We start by making a new object called VotingClassifier, which is a hybrid of the Random Forest and SVM classifiers. A list of tuples, each of which consisting of a string identifier and an object classifier, is what we send along as our input. The terms "rf" and "svm" will serve as the identifiers in this scenario. By utilizing the fit() method, we train the VotingClassifier using the provided data. Both the Random Forest and SVM classifiers are trained because of this. We use the predict() method to generate predictions on the testing data in order to evaluate the effectiveness of the hybrid model. We determine an accuracy score by contrasting the labels that are anticipated with the labels that appear. See Figure 4.9 for the code snippet.

4.4.2 Random Forest + k-NN

Next, we use the K neighbors Classifier class provided by scikit-learn to generate an instance of the k-NN classifier. We make a new instance of the VotingClassifier object that uses a classification strategy that mixes Random Forest and k-NN. We train the VotingClassifier using the provided data. Based on the testing results, we formulate hypotheses and then compute an accuracy score. Refer to Figure 4.10 for the code snippet.

4.4.3 SVM + k-NN

In a similar manner, we create an object called VotingClassifier that integrates both the SVM and the k-NN classifiers. We train the VotingClassifier using the provided data. Based on the testing results, we formulate hypotheses and then compute an accuracy score (see Figure 4.11).

```
scaler = StandardScaler() #creates an instance of the StandardScaler class from the scikit-learn preprocessing module.
#the fit_transform() method of the StandardScaler object to scale (i.e. standardize) the training features in 'X_train'.
#This involves centering the data (i.e. subtracting the mean) and scaling it (i.e. dividing by the standard deviation) so that each feature has a mean of 0 and a standard deviation of 1.
X_train = scaler.fit_transform(X_train)
#the transform() method of the StandardScaler object to scale the test features in 'X_test'.
#Importantly, we only call transform() on the test data, and not fit_transform().
#This is because we want to use the same scaling factors learned from the training data to scale the test data, so that the test data is not used to influence the scaling process.
X_test = scaler.transform(X_test)
```

Figure 4.8 Code snippet to use the StandardScaler tool.

```
# Train a Random Forest + SVM model

#creates an instance of the RandomForestClassifier class from the scikit-learn ensemble module.
#The 'n_estimators' parameter specifies the number of trees in the random forest, and 'random_state' sets the seed for the random number generator.
rf = RandomForestClassifier(n_estimators=100, random_state=0)
#creates an instance of the SVC (Support Vector Classifier) class from the scikit-learn svm module.
#The 'kernel' parameter specifies the type of kernel to use in the SVM algorithm (in this case, a linear kernel), and 'C' specifies the penalty parameter of the error term in the SVM objective function
#The 'random_state' parameter sets the seed for the random number generator.
svm = SVC(kernel='linear', C=1.0, random_state=0)
#creates an instance of the VotingClassifier class from the ensemble module.
#The 'estimators' parameter is a list of (name, estimator) pairs, where each estimator is a machine learning model that will be combined using the specified voting method ('hard' voting in this case).
rf_svm = VotingClassifier(estimators=[('rf', rf), ('svm', svm)], voting='hard')
rf_svm.fit(X_train, y_train)#fits the voting classifier to the training data using the fit() method.
rf_svm_acc = rf_svm.score(X_test, y_test)#calculates the accuracy of the voting classifier on the test data using the score() method.
rf_svm_acc #returns the calculated accuracy of the voting classifier on the test data.

0.9649122807017544
```

Figure 4.9 Training a Random Forest + SVM Model.

```
# Train a Random Forest + k-NN Model
#creates an instance of the RandomForestClassifier class from the scikit-learn ensemble module.
#The 'n_estimators' parameter specifies the number of trees in the random forest, and 'random_state' sets the seed for the random number generator.
rf = RandomForestClassifier(n_estimators=100, random_state=0)
# creates an instance of the KNeighborsClassifier class from the scikit-learn neighbors module
#The 'n_neighbors' parameter specifies the number of neighbors to consider, 'metric' specifies the distance metric to use (in this case, the Minkowski distance), and 'p' specifies the power parameter for the Minkowski distance.
knn = KNeighborsClassifier(n_neighbors=5, metric='minkowski', p=2)
#creates an instance of the VotingClassifier class from the ensemble module.
#The 'estimators' parameter is a list of (name, estimator) pairs, where each estimator is a machine learning model that will be combined using the specified voting method ('hard' voting in this case).
rf_knn = VotingClassifier(estimators=[('rf', rf), ('knn', knn)], voting='hard')
rf_knn.fit(X_train, y_train)#fits the voting classifier to the training data using the fit() method.
rf_knn_acc = rf_knn.score(X_test, y_test)#calculates the accuracy of the voting classifier on the test data using the score() method.
rf_knn_acc#returns the calculated accuracy of the voting classifier on the test data.

0.9561403508771193
```

Figure 4.10 Training a Random Forest + k-NN Model.

```
# Train a SVM + k-NN model
#creates an instance of the SVC class from the scikit-learn svm module.
#The 'kernel' parameter specifies the type of kernel function to be used ('linear' in this case), 'C' is the regularization parameter, and 'random_state' sets the seed for the random number generator.
svm = SVC(kernel='linear', C=1.0, random_state=0)
#creates an instance of the KNeighborsClassifier class from the scikit-learn neighbors module. The 'n_neighbors' parameter specifies the number of neighbors to consider (1 in this case),
# 'metric' specifies the distance metric to use (in this case, the Minkowski distance), and 'p' specifies the power parameter for the Minkowski distance.
knn = KNeighborsClassifier(n_neighbors=1, metric='minkowski', p=2)
#creates an instance of the VotingClassifier class from the ensemble module. The 'estimators' parameter is a list of (name, estimator) pairs,
# where each estimator is a machine learning model that will be combined using the specified voting method ('hard' voting in this case).
svm_knn = VotingClassifier(estimators=[('svm', svm), ('knn', knn)], voting='hard')
# fits the voting classifier to the training data using the fit() method.
svm_knn.fit(X_train, y_train)
# -calculates the accuracy of the voting classifier on the test data using the score() method.
svm_knn_acc = svm_knn.score(X_test, y_test)
# returns the calculated accuracy of the voting classifier on the test data.
svm_knn_acc

0.9473684210526315
```

Figure 4.11 Training a SVM + k-NN Model.

4.5 CONCLUSION

This chapter focused on creating hybrid machine learning models, which we have discussed in depth. We have gained the knowledge necessary to preprocess the data, develop hybrid models by utilizing various combinations of classifiers, and evaluate the effectiveness of these models. We can increase the accuracy of our predictions as well as make use of the specific characteristics of each of the models by combining them. The information that has been learned in this chapter can be put to use when developing your own hybrid models for use in a variety of machine learning applications.

4.6 FURTHER LEARNING

Exploring feature-engineering techniques, conducting hyper parameter tuning, selecting appropriate base models, conducting experiments with applying cross-validation, and testing the model in real-life situations are some of the upcoming works and enhancements for hybrid machine-learning models. These efforts focus on enhancing the model's performance, resilience, generalization ability, and practical usability, with the end goal of making it more effective at resolving complex issues across a variety of application areas.

SUGGESTED READINGS

Atallah, D.M., Badawy, M., El-Sayed, A. and Ghoneim, M.A., 2019. Predicting kidney transplantation outcome based on hybrid feature selection and KNN classifier. *Multimedia Tools and Applications*, 78, pp.20383–20407.

Demidova, L., Nikulchev, E. and Sokolova, Y., 2016. The SVM classifier based on the modified particle swarm optimization. *arXiv*, 1603.08296.

Gislason, P.O., Benediktsson, J.A. and Sveinsson, J.R., 2006. Random forests for land cover classification. *Pattern Recognition Letters*, 27(4), pp.294–300.

Kavitha, M., Gnaneswar, G., Dinesh, R., Sai, Y.R. and Suraj, R.S., 2021, January. Heart disease prediction using hybrid machine learning model. In *2021 6th International Conference on Inventive Computation Technologies (ICICT)* (pp.1329–1333). IEEE.

Chapter 5

Flower recognition with Kaggle dataset and Gradio interface

LEARNING OBJECTIVES

By the end of this chapter, the reader shall be able to:

- Acquire the knowledge to construct a machine learning model that can divide photographs into several distinct groups.
- Obtain predictions based on their own models.
- Integrate Gradio, a user-friendly interface library.

5.1 INTRODUCTION

We will use a dataset collected from Kaggle to explore the fascinating realm of flower recognition in this chapter. Flower recognition is a field that has been studied for centuries. Readers will get the knowledge necessary to construct a machine learning model that is able to divide photographs of flowers into five distinct groups by following the instructions provided. The procedure of immediately obtaining datasets from Kaggle, without the need for manual downloads, will be covered in this chapter, setting it apart from the others in the book and making it the focal point of what makes this chapter unique. In addition, we are going to investigate the possibility of integrating Gradio, which is a user-friendly interface library. Gradio gives users the ability to engage using the model and obtain predictions based on their own photographs of flowers. Readers will have received practical insights into image categorization, dataset collecting, and interacting with users with machine learning models by the time they reach the end of this chapter.

5.2 DOWNLOADING THE DATASET

The manual downloading and preparation of data has always been a necessary step in the process of getting datasets from external sources. On the other hand, we shall present the readers with a method that is more streamlined in this

DOI: 10.1201/9781032676685-6

chapter. We no longer need to manually download the "flowers-recognition" dataset because we can immediately grab it from Kaggle using the OpenDatasets library instead of doing so manually. The process of data collecting is not only sped up because of this, but it also saves time.

Once you are done installing the necessary libraries as in Figure 5.1, follow these steps.

Step 1: Go to www.kaggle.com/
Step 2: Choose the dataset (in this chapter we used the flower recognition dataset).
Step 3: Copy the link www.kaggle.com/datasets/alxmamaev/flowers-recognition

You can see we have used our dataset link in the above code as seen in Figure 5.2. As a next step, you will have to enter your Kaggle username and key once after executing the above code. Follow the steps mentioned below for your Kaggle username and key.

Step 1: You can access your Kaggle account by going to the website www.kaggle.com/ and logging in there. Create an account for yourself if you do not already have one.
Step 2: After you have successfully logged in, navigate to the settings page for your account. You can access your Kaggle account by going to the top right corner of the website, clicking on your profile image, and then selecting "My Account" from the dropdown menu.
Step 3: To generate a new API token, scroll down until you reach the section labeled "API," then click the option that says "Create New API Token." This will cause a file with the name kaggle.json to be downloaded on your computer. It will contain your API credentials.

5.3 DATA PREPROCESSING

These lines of code as in Figure 5.3 will load the necessary libraries in order to build the machine learning model using TensorFlow, which involves data handling and visualization.

In this step, we will determine the image size and set the path to the dataset. The path to the dataset downloaded is stored in the data_dir variable, which has its value set to that path. img_height and img_width are the two parameters that indicate the length and width of the images being used and will be adjusted when the model is trained. Refer to Figure 5.4 for the code snippet.

```
%pip install opendatasets
%pip install pandas

Looking in indexes: https://pypi.org/simple, https://us-python.pkg.dev/colab-wheels/public/simple/
Collecting opendatasets
  Downloading opendatasets-0.1.22-py3-none-any.whl (15 kB)
Requirement already satisfied: click in /usr/local/lib/python3.10/dist-packages (from opendatasets) (8.1.3)
Requirement already satisfied: tqdm in /usr/local/lib/python3.10/dist-packages (from opendatasets) (4.65.0)
Requirement already satisfied: kaggle in /usr/local/lib/python3.10/dist-packages (from opendatasets) (1.5.13)
Requirement already satisfied: certifi in /usr/local/lib/python3.10/dist-packages (from kaggle->opendatasets) (2022.12.7)
Requirement already satisfied: python-dateutil in /usr/local/lib/python3.10/dist-packages (from kaggle->opendatasets) (2.8.2)
Requirement already satisfied: python-slugify in /usr/local/lib/python3.10/dist-packages (from kaggle->opendatasets) (8.0.1)
Requirement already satisfied: six>=1.10 in /usr/local/lib/python3.10/dist-packages (from kaggle->opendatasets) (1.16.0)
Requirement already satisfied: requests in /usr/local/lib/python3.10/dist-packages (from kaggle->opendatasets) (2.27.1)
Requirement already satisfied: urllib3 in /usr/local/lib/python3.10/dist-packages (from kaggle->opendatasets) (1.26.15)
Requirement already satisfied: text-unidecode>=1.3 in /usr/local/lib/python3.10/dist-packages (from python-slugify->kaggle->opendatasets) (1.3)
Requirement already satisfied: charset-normalizer~=2.0.0 in /usr/local/lib/python3.10/dist-packages (from requests->kaggle->opendatasets) (2.0.12)
Requirement already satisfied: idna<4,>=2.5 in /usr/local/lib/python3.10/dist-packages (from requests->kaggle->opendatasets) (3.4)
Installing collected packages: opendatasets
Successfully installed opendatasets-0.1.22
Looking in indexes: https://pypi.org/simple, https://us-python.pkg.dev/colab-wheels/public/simple/
Requirement already satisfied: pandas in /usr/local/lib/python3.10/dist-packages (1.5.3)
Requirement already satisfied: numpy>=1.21.0 in /usr/local/lib/python3.10/dist-packages (from pandas) (1.22.4)
Requirement already satisfied: pytz>=2020.1 in /usr/local/lib/python3.10/dist-packages (from pandas) (2022.7.1)
Requirement already satisfied: python-dateutil>=2.8.1 in /usr/local/lib/python3.10/dist-packages (from pandas) (2.8.2)
Requirement already satisfied: six>=1.5 in /usr/local/lib/python3.10/dist-packages (from python-dateutil>=2.8.1->pandas) (1.16.0)
```

Figure 5.1 Installing necessary libraries.

```
import opendatasets as od
import pandas

od.download(
  "https://www.kaggle.com/datasets/alxmamaev/flowers-recognition")

Please provide your Kaggle credentials to download this dataset. Learn more: http://bit.ly/kaggle-creds
Your Kaggle username: akshayramakrishnan28
Your Kaggle Key: ··········
Downloading flowers-recognition.zip to ./flowers-recognition
100%|██████████| 225M/225M [00:06<00:00, 38.7MB/s]
```

Figure 5.2 Importing the datasets.

```
# Import necessary libraries
import os
import numpy as np
import pandas as pd
import matplotlib.pyplot as plt
import tensorflow as tf
from tensorflow.keras.preprocessing.image import ImageDataGenerator
```

Figure 5.3 Code snippet to import libraries.

```
# Set the path to the dataset
data_dir = '/content/flowers-recognition/flowers'

# Define the image dimensions and batch size
img_height = 224
img_width = 224
batch_size = 32
```

Figure 5.4 Code snippet for image size and path setting.

5.4 CREATING THE MODEL ARCHITECTURE

In order to enrich the available data, we create an ImageDataGenerator as shown in Figure 5.5. TensorFlow's ImageDataGenerator is a utility class that assists with data enhancement and data preprocessing. It may also be used to generate image data. The changes that are going to be applied to the photos, such as resizing, cutting, enlargement, and horizontally flipping the images, are defined by the parameters that are supplied in this section.

```
# Create an ImageDataGenerator for data augmentation
train_datagen = ImageDataGenerator(
    rescale=1./255,
    shear_range=0.2,
    zoom_range=0.2,
    horizontal_flip=True,
    validation_split=0.2
)
```

Figure 5.5 Code snippet for image data generation.

```
# Load the training data from the directory using the ImageDataGenerator
train_data = train_datagen.flow_from_directory(
    data_dir,
    target_size=(img_height, img_width),
    batch_size=batch_size,
    class_mode='categorical',
    subset='training'
)
```

Found 3457 images belonging to 5 classes.

Figure 5.6 Code snippet for loading training data.

```
# Load the validation data from the directory using the ImageDataGenerator
val_data = train_datagen.flow_from_directory(
    data_dir,
    target_size=(img_height, img_width),
    batch_size=batch_size,
    class_mode='categorical',
    subset='validation'
)
```

Found 860 images belonging to 5 classes.

Figure 5.7 Code snippet for loading validation data.

These lines as in Figure 5.6 and Figure 5.7 utilize the flow_from_directory function of the ImageDataGenerator in order to load the training data and validation data respectively from the directory specified.

The photographs are shrunk down to the goal size set, and the batch size is what decides the number of images that are worked on during each

```
# Define the model architecture
model = tf.keras.Sequential([
    tf.keras.layers.Conv2D(32, (3, 3), activation='relu', input_shape=(img_height, img_width, 3)),
    tf.keras.layers.MaxPooling2D((2, 2)),
    tf.keras.layers.Conv2D(64, (3, 3), activation='relu'),
    tf.keras.layers.MaxPooling2D((2, 2)),
    tf.keras.layers.Conv2D(128, (3, 3), activation='relu'),
    tf.keras.layers.MaxPooling2D((2, 2)),
    tf.keras.layers.Flatten(),
    tf.keras.layers.Dense(128, activation='relu'),
    tf.keras.layers.Dropout(0.5),
    tf.keras.layers.Dense(5, activation='softmax')
])
```

Figure 5.8 Code snippet to define model architecture.

iteration. Since we will be working with multi-class categorization, the class_mode is set to the categorical setting. The subset parameter is utilized to divide the data into the training set and the validation set according to the validation split that has been given.

5.5 TRAINING THE MODEL

The code provided in Figure 5.8 defines the structure of the model used for deep learning, which makes use of the Sequential API that TensorFlow provides. The model is made up of convolutional layers, followed by max pooling layers for the purpose of feature extraction. Flattening the output of the maximum pooling layer that came before it and then connecting it to a dense layer that uses ReLU activation completes the process. A dropout layer added to the network prevents overfitting, and the final dense layer using softmax activation generates the class probabilities.

The Adam optimizer, the categorical cross-entropy loss function, and the accuracy metric are used in the compilation of the model. In order to train the model with the help of the training data for a predetermined amount of epochs, the fit technique is invoked. The performance of the model is assessed during the training process based on the validation data (see Figure 5.9).

5.6 DEVELOPING AN INTERFACE BASED ON GRADIO

The code snippet for function definition to make predictions on the input images is presented in Figure 5.10. We will make use of the Gradio library in order to develop an intuitive interface for flower recognition. Gradio enables us to define machine learning models' interfaces in a straightforward manner. We are going to build a user interface that, after receiving an image as input, displays the type of flower present.

```
# Compile the model with appropriate loss and optimizer
model.compile(
    optimizer='adam',
    loss='categorical_crossentropy',
    metrics=['accuracy']
)

# Train the model on the training data
history = model.fit(
    train_data,
    epochs=2,
    validation_data=val_data
)

Epoch 1/2
109/109 [==============================] - 557s 5s/step - loss: 1.4323 - accuracy: 0.3951 - val_loss: 1.1927 - val_accuracy: 0.4895
Epoch 2/2
109/109 [==============================] - 498s 5s/step - loss: 1.1509 - accuracy: 0.5314 - val_loss: 1.1267 - val_accuracy: 0.5547
```

Figure 5.9 Code snippet for model compilation.

```
# Define a function to make predictions on input images
def classify_flower(image):
    image = tf.image.resize(image, (img_height, img_width))
    image = image / 255.0
    prediction = model.predict(np.array([image]))
    class_names = ['daisy', 'dandelion', 'rose', 'sunflower', 'tulip']
    return {class_names[i]: float(prediction[0][i]) for i in range(5)}
```

Figure 5.10 Code snippet for function definition.

Importing the Gradio library results in the definition of a function called classify_flower, which is used to categorize the input image of a flower. In order to determine the probabilities that will be predicted, the function will first resize the image, then normalize it, and then run it through the trained model.

gr.Interface is used to design the interface, with an image and a label being specified as the input and output respectively. The example photos, as well as the interface's title and description, are presented here for your perusal. The Gradio interface is launched when the code iface.launch() is executed. This gives users the ability to interact with the flower categorization model using their own photos. See Figure 5.11.

Note: If the gradio module is not already present in the environment you are working in, you may get it by running the following code: % pip install gradio.

The Figure 5.12 is an example interface that we created using Gradio.

5.7 CONCLUSION

Using a dataset from Kaggle, we can reach the fascinating conclusion that flower recognition is a worthwhile endeavor to investigate. We are able to train a convolutional neural network (CNN) model by utilizing the power of deep learning and TensorFlow. This model is capable of classifying flower photos into the following five distinct categories: daisy, dandelion, rose, sunflower, and tulip. We also familiarize the readers with Gradio, a library that is friendly to users and designed for the creation of interactive interfaces. Gradio gives users the ability to identify photographs of flowers by using a model that has been developed.

The readers have learnt how to construct and train a CNN model for flower recognition, as well as how to create a Gradio interface for real-time predictions, by following the step-by-step instructions and downloading a dataset directly from Kaggle using the opendatasets package. The readers also learned how to preprocess the data using the ImageDataGenerator

```
# Create the Gradio interface
import gradio as gr
iface = gr.Interface(
    fn=classify_flower,
    inputs=gr.inputs.Image(),
    outputs=gr.outputs.Label(num_top_classes=5),
    title='Flower Classifier',
    description='Classify images of flowers into 5 different categories.'
    examples=[
        ['path/to/example/image.jpg'],
        ['path/to/another/example/image.jpg']
    ]
)


# Launch the interface
iface.launch()


100%|███████████| 764/764 [00:02<00:00, 311.86it/s]764
```

Figure 5.11 Importing the Gradio library.

class. This chapter gave a complete overview of the end-to-end process of constructing a flower recognition system. As a result, readers are sure to obtain hands-on experience with deep learning and model deployment. Moreover, the chapter has also discussed the benefits of using such a system.

5.8 FURTHER LEARNING

Flower recognition has many possible improvements. By adapting pre-trained models to flower recognition, adjusting and transferable learning can be studied. This method may increase model accuracy and generalization. Second, grid-based and random searches can be used to optimize learning percentage, batch quantity, and network architecture. Model performance can also increase. Third, the methods of scaling, rotation, and random cropping can be employed to diversify and strengthen the training dataset. Fourth, adding more flower species to the dataset can improve the model's recognition abilities. Finally, putting the model to a web-based app can allows users to contribute flower photos and receive predictions in real time. Improved model accuracy, dataset diversity, and user involvement and accessibility will improve flower recognition.

Figure 5.12 Created Gradio interfaces.

SUGGESTED READINGS

Bharati, P. and Pramanik, A., 2020. Deep learning techniques—R-CNN to mask R-CNN: A survey. In *Computational Intelligence in Pattern Recognition: Proceedings of CIPR 2019* (pp.657–668). Springer Singapore.

Python library for easily interacting with trained machine learning models, gradio 4.19.2 https://pypi.org/project/gradio/

Chapter 6

Drug classification with hyperparameter tuning

LEARNING OBJECTIVES

After completing this chapter, the reader shall be able to:

- Acquire essential knowledge into the method of hyperparameter tuning as well as how it may dramatically increase the accuracy and efficacy of machine learning models.
- Understand the significance of hyperparameter tuning and to implement it into K-Nearest Neighbors (KNN), Multilayer Perceptron (MLP), and Random Forest (RF) models.

6.1 INTRODUCTION

In this chapter, we will look into the interesting area of drug identification and classification and investigate the methodologies of hyperparameter tuning in order to improve the overall performance of our models. The idea of hyperparameters, as well as the critical part they play in the optimization of models, will be presented here. In addition, we will investigate the capabilities of GridSearchCV, which is a potent application that helps automate the process of determining the optimal values for hyperparameters by conducting an exhaustive search across the parameter space. The implementation in K-Nearest Neighbors (KNN), Multilayer Perceptron (MLP), and Random Forest (RF) models through the use of practical examples and the development of code is provided. This chapter's goal is to provide you with the information and skills required to optimize the models and reveal the full potential that they possess.

6.2 DATA PREPROCESSING AND SPLITTING

Let's begin by importing the necessary libraries for our job. We import the pandas library for data manipulation, the train_test_split function from scikit-learn for splitting the dataset, the StandardScaler function from

DOI: 10.1201/9781032676685-7

```
import pandas as pd  # Importing pandas library for data manipulation
import matplotlib.pyplot as plt  # Importing matplotlib library for data visualization
from sklearn.model_selection import train_test_split, GridSearchCV  # Importing functions for data splitting and grid search
from sklearn.ensemble import RandomForestClassifier  # Importing Random Forest classifier
from sklearn.neighbors import KNeighborsClassifier  # Importing K-Nearest Neighbors classifier
from sklearn.neural_network import MLPClassifier  # Importing Multilayer Perceptron classifier
from sklearn.metrics import accuracy_score  # Importing accuracy score for model evaluation
```

Figure 6.1 Code snippet for importing the needed libraries.

```
# Load the drug classification dataset from Kaggle
data = pd.read_csv('/content/drug200.csv')
```

Figure 6.2 Code snippet for loading the dataset.

scikit-learn for feature scaling, KNeighborsClassifier, MLPClassifier, and RandomForestClassifier for the respective models, GridSearchCV to provide hyperparameter tuning, and different metrics from scikit-learn for model evaluation. In addition, we bring in the matplotlib.pyplot library so that we can visualize the data. See Figure 6.1.

We import the drug categorization dataset via a CSV file by utilizing the read_csv function that is available in pandas, and then we save it to the variable known as data, as seen in Figure 6.2.

We use the head() function to look at the first five rows from the data frame to get some basic inference on the data. Something to notice here is columns "Sex," "BP," and "Cholesterol" contains categorical variables. We can see our data frame has six columns and Drug is our target column. Next we check for the null values – we don't have any missing values in our dataset. See Figure 6.3.

In the first step of our data analysis, called preprocessing as seen in Figure 6.4, we transform categorical variables into numbers and then normalize the numerical features. We execute one-hot encoding on the categorical values present in our dataset such as "Sex," "BP," and "Cholesterol" by utilizing the function get_dummies that is available in the pandas library. This gives them a corresponding representation in numerical form.

In order to train the model, we first separate the preprocessed data into its features (X) and then into its target variable (y) as given in Figure 6.5. We give the preprocessed features (every column other than "Drug") to the variable "X," and we give the target parameter ("Drug") to the constant "y."

When dividing the data into training and testing sets, we make use of the train_test_split function that is included in the scikit-learn package. The "test_size" argument allows the user to specify the percentage of the dataset that will be utilized for testing, and the "random_state" parameter assures

```
data.head()
```

	Age	Sex	BP	Cholesterol	Na_to_K	Drug
0	23	F	HIGH	HIGH	25.355	DrugY
1	47	M	LOW	HIGH	13.093	drugC
2	47	M	LOW	HIGH	10.114	drugC
3	28	F	NORMAL	HIGH	7.798	drugX
4	61	F	LOW	HIGH	18.043	DrugY

```
data.isnull().sum()

Age            0
Sex            0
BP             0
Cholesterol    0
Na_to_K        0
Drug           0
dtype: int64
```

Figure 6.3 Getting inference on the data.

```
# Preprocess the data
# Convert categorical variables to numerical using one-hot encoding
data = pd.get_dummies(data, columns=['Sex', 'BP', 'Cholesterol'])
```

Figure 6.4 Code snippet for Data preprocessing.

```
# Split the data into features (X) and target variable (y)
X = data.drop('Drug', axis=1)
y = data['Drug']
```

Figure 6.5 Code snippet for splitting the data.

```
# Split the data into training and testing sets
X_train, X_test, y_train, y_test = train_test_split(X, y, test_size=0.2, random_state=42)
```

Figure 6.6 Code snippet for data separation.

```
# Create a Random Forest classifier for drug classification
rf_classifier = RandomForestClassifier()

# Create a K-Nearest Neighbors classifier for drug classification
knn_classifier = KNeighborsClassifier()

# Create a Multilayer Perceptron classifier for drug classification
mlp_classifier = MLPClassifier()
```

Figure 6.7 Code snippet for classifiers.

that the random seed will always be the same, which ensures repeatability. See Figure 6.6.

6.3 MODELING

The preceding piece of code generates instances of three different classifiers for the purpose of drug categorization. These classifiers are referred to as above in Figure 6.7. The Random Forest classifier is a combination of several decision trees, the KNN classifier assigns scores depending on the degree to which neighbors are similar to one another, and the MLP classifier is a neural network with multiple layers that are connected to one another.

6.4 HYPERPARAMETER TUNING

The code snippet to define the hyperparameter grid for grid search for each classifier is given in Figure 6.8. In order to identify the optimal combination for the RF classifier, we use GridSearchCV to search through an input parameter grid that includes values for "n_estimators," "max_ depth," and "criterion." Our goal is to locate the parameter values that produce the most accurate results. In a similar manner, we modify the "n_neighbors" hyperparameter for the KNN classifier by using GridSearchCV. This allows us to evaluate the performance of the model

```
# Define the hyperparameter grid for grid search for each classifier
rf_param_grid = {
    'n_estimators': [100, 200, 300],
    'max_depth': [None, 5, 10],
    'min_samples_split': [2, 5, 10]
}

knn_param_grid = {
    'n_neighbors': [3, 5, 7],
    'weights': ['uniform', 'distance']
}

mlp_param_grid = {
    'hidden_layer_sizes': [(50,), (100,), (50, 50)],
    'activation': ['relu', 'tanh'],
    'solver': ['adam', 'sgd']
}
```

Figure 6.8 Code snippet to define the hyperparameter grid.

```
# Perform grid search to find the best hyperparameters for each classifier
rf_grid_search = GridSearchCV(rf_classifier, rf_param_grid, cv=5)
knn_grid_search = GridSearchCV(knn_classifier, knn_param_grid, cv=5)
mlp_grid_search = GridSearchCV(mlp_classifier, mlp_param_grid, cv=5)

rf_grid_search.fit(X_train, y_train)
knn_grid_search.fit(X_train, y_train)
mlp_grid_search.fit(X_train, y_train)
```

Figure 6.9 Code snippet to perform grid search.

with a variety of neighbor values. In the instance of the MLP classifier, we concentrate on tuning hyperparameters such as "hidden_layer_sizes," "activation," and "max_iter" in order to improve the design of the neural network. We automate the search for the best possible hyperparameters by utilizing GridSearchCV, which also helps to improve the accuracy of the models and their overall performance in drug categorization tasks. See Figure 6.9.

We have three different models, thus in order to determine the optimal combination of hyperparameters for each of them, we utilize GridSearchCV.

We first fit the grid search object to the training data, and then we obtain the best hyperparameters, which we then save in the variable named "modelname_best_params" correspondingly for all three of the models that we have employed. Refer to Figure 6.10 for the code snippet.

6.5 MODEL TRAINING AND EVALUATION

Using the three models that have been trained, we generate predictions using the testing data as in Figure 6.11.

Calculating the model's accuracy with the scikit-learn functions that correspond to that calculation allows us to assess the performance of the model. Refer to Figure 6.12 for the code snippet.

We then move on to printing the accuracy of our respective models. Refer to Figure 6.13 for the code snippet.

6.6 MODEL COMPARISON AND VISUALIZATION

A line chart is developed so that we can examine the degrees of accuracy achieved by each of the three models. The "models" listed in Figure 6.14

```
# Get the best hyperparameter values and the corresponding best models
rf_best_params = rf_grid_search.best_params_
knn_best_params = knn_grid_search.best_params_
mlp_best_params = mlp_grid_search.best_params_

rf_best_model = rf_grid_search.best_estimator_
knn_best_model = knn_grid_search.best_estimator_
mlp_best_model = mlp_grid_search.best_estimator_
```

Figure 6.10 Code snippet to get the best hyperparameter value.

```
# Make predictions on the test set using the best models
rf_y_pred = rf_best_model.predict(X_test)
knn_y_pred = knn_best_model.predict(X_test)
mlp_y_pred = mlp_best_model.predict(X_test)
```

Figure 6.11 Code snippet to generate predictions on the test set.

```
# Calculate the accuracy of each drug classification model
rf_accuracy = accuracy_score(y_test, rf_y_pred)
knn_accuracy = accuracy_score(y_test, knn_y_pred)
mlp_accuracy = accuracy_score(y_test, mlp_y_pred)
```

Figure 6.12 Code snippet to calculate accuracy.

```
# Calculate the accuracy of each drug classification model
print("Random Forest Accuracy:", rf_accuracy)
print("K-Nearest Neighbors Accuracy:", knn_accuracy)
print("Multilayer Perceptron Accuracy:", mlp_accuracy)

Random Forest Accuracy: 0.87
K-Nearest Neighbors Accuracy: 0.75
Multilayer Perceptron Accuracy: 0.925
```

Figure 6.13 Code snippet to print the accuracy.

```
# Create a line chart to compare the accuracy of the models
models = ['Random Forest', 'K-Nearest Neighbors', 'Multilayer Perceptron']
accuracies = [rf_accuracy, knn_accuracy, mlp_accuracy]

plt.plot(models, accuracies, marker='o')
plt.xlabel('Models')
plt.ylabel('Accuracy')
plt.title('Accuracy Comparison of Drug Classification Models')
plt.ylim([0, 1])
plt.grid(True)
plt.show()
```

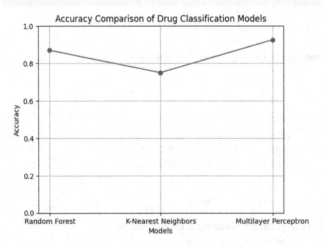

Figure 6.14 Accuracy Comparison.

includes the names of the models ("KNN," "MLP," and "RF"), and the "accuracies" list includes the accuracies that correspond to those models. When plotting the line chart, we define markers, linestyle, and color before passing the data to the plot function found in matplotlib.pyplot. We determine the title, the label for the x-axis, the label for the y-axis, and the limitations for the y-axis.

In the end, we show the line chart by using the plt.show() function.

6.7 CONCLUSION

In this chapter, we have classified drugs using KNN, MLP, and RF models, and tuned their hyperparameters using various hyperparameter tuning strategies. We improved the performance of the models by locating the hyperparameters that worked best for them. The line chart comparison highlighted the disparities in accuracy that existed between the models, thereby shedding light on the efficiency of their respective approaches. The process of adjusting hyperparameters is an essential stage in the optimization of machine learning models, and it can considerably improve the latter's capacity for prediction.

6.8 FURTHER LEARNING

In this chapter, we looked into the classification of drugs utilizing a wide variety of models and approaches for adjusting hyperparameters. Nevertheless, there are a lot of other directions this work and progress could go in the future. For a more effective search as well as greater exploration of the hyperparameter space, it is possible to make use of more sophisticated methods for tuning hyperparameters, such as Bayesian optimization or genetic algorithms. Additional study could concentrate on feature engineering in order to improve the depiction of the drug categorization dataset. This could involve investigating various strategies for dimensionality reduction or the incorporation of domain-specific information. Stacking and boosting are two examples of ensemble approaches that can be used to aggregate the predictions of numerous models in order to achieve a higher level of accuracy in classification. Problems with class imbalance can be remedied by employing techniques such as oversampling and under sampling, or SMOTE (Synthetic Minority Oversampling Technique) to deal with imbalanced data. When dealing with drug classification challenges, it may be beneficial to investigate deep learning methodologies such as convolutional neural networks and recurrent neural networks also.

SUGGESTED READINGS

Altay, O., Ulas, M. and Alyamac, K.E., 2020. Prediction of the fresh performance of steel fiber reinforced self-compacting concrete using quadratic SVM and weighted KNN models. *IEEE Access, 8*, pp.92647–92658.

Mangkunegara, I.S. and Purwono, P., 2022, June. Analysis of DNA sequence classification using SVM model with hyperparameter tuning grid search CV. In *2022 IEEE International Conference on Cybernetics and Computational Intelligence (CyberneticsCom)* (pp. 427–432). IEEE.

Passos, D. and Mishra, P., 2022. A tutorial on automatic hyperparameter tuning of deep spectral modelling for regression and classification tasks. *Chemometrics and Intelligent Laboratory Systems, 223*, 104520.

Rodriguez-Galiano, V.F., Ghimire, B., Rogan, J., Chica-Olmo, M. and Rigol-Sanchez, J.P., 2012. An assessment of the effectiveness of a random forest classifier for land-cover classification. *ISPRS Journal of Photogrammetry and Remote Sensing, 67*, pp.93–104.

Windeatt, T., 2008. Ensemble MLP classifier design. In *Computational Intelligence Paradigms: Innovative Applications* (pp.133–147). Springer.

Chapter 7

Evaluating model performance

Metrics for diabetes prediction

LEARNING OBJECTIVES

After completing this chapter, the reader shall be able to:

- Forecast diabetes using machine learning methods.
- Analyze the efficiency of the models by means of performance metrics evaluation.

7.1 INTRODUCTION

In this chapter, we will go into the task of forecasting diabetes using machine learning methods on the Pima Indians Diabetes Database. The data for this chapter comes from the Pima Indians Diabetes Database obtained from kaggle. Users can obtain the dataset from the following link: www.kaggle. com/datasets/uciml/pima-indians-diabetes-database. We have an intriguing new addition for our readers that builds on the foundation laid in our prior chapters. In this chapter, we will analyze the efficiency of our models by discussing the notion of performance metrics, which will be introduced here. You will gain an understanding of a variety of metrics that provide a more in-depth insight of the performance of models, going beyond the concept of simple accuracy. Let's jump right in and start learning about the performance assessment world!

7.2 PERFORMANCE METRICS

In the field of machine learning, it is essential to conduct performance evaluations of our models in order to have an understanding of how well these models are carrying out the task at hand. Although accuracy is a popular metric, it might not give a whole picture of how effective the model is. In this section, we are going to introduce numerous performance indicators or metrics that provide us with the ability to evaluate various elements of the model's performance. Let's look at each metric in more detail:

DOI: 10.1201/9781032676685-8

Accuracy: It is a measure of the overall accuracy of predictions, and indicates the proportion of correctly classified examples relative to the total number of occurrences. Accuracy assesses the overall correctness of forecasts. Accuracy is a valuable indicator, but it may not be sufficient when working with datasets that are imbalanced or when the cost of misclassification changes across various classes.

Precision: Precision refers to the ratio of accurately anticipated positive cases (true positives) to the total number of predicted positive cases (true positives plus false positives). Because it evaluates the model's capacity to avoid producing false positives, precision is especially important in situations in which the identification of positive cases is of paramount importance.

Recall (Sensitivity): Recall, which is also known as sensitivity or true positive rate, measures the proportion of actual positive cases properly detected by the model (true positives) out of the total number of genuine positive cases (true positives plus false negatives). When the objective is to identify as many true positive cases as possible while reducing the number of false negatives, recall is an indispensable tool.

Score of F1: The F1 score is a fair evaluation of the model's performance because it combines precision and recall into a single statistic. It is the harmonic mean of precision and recall, taking into account both false positives and false negatives. It is a measure of diagnostic accuracy. The F1 score can range from 0 to 1, with 1 reflecting flawless precision and recall.

ROC AUC Score: The Receiver Operating Characteristic (ROC) curve is an illustration of the model's performance at various categorization criteria. The model's ability to differentiate between positive and negative classes is quantified by a score known as the Area Under the ROC Curve (ROC AUC). Indicative of more discriminative capacity is a ROC AUC value that is higher.

By making use of these performance indicators, we are able to achieve a more in-depth comprehension of the strengths and shortcomings possessed by our models with regard to the diabetes prediction. With the help of these measures, we are able to examine specific features in addition to general accuracy, such as recall and precision, as well as the balance between the two. Let's move on with our investigation and use these metrics to evaluate how well various machine learning models perform on the Pima Indians Diabetes dataset.

7.3 DATA PRE-PROCESSING

The lines of code as seen in Figure 7.1 provide import necessary libraries and modules that will be used for the tasks of data manipulation, evaluation,

```
# Importing Libraries and Loading the Data
import pandas as pd  # Import pandas library for data manipulation
import numpy as np  # Import numpy library for numerical operations
from sklearn.model_selection import train_test_split  # Import train_test_split function for data splitting
from sklearn.preprocessing import StandardScaler  # Import StandardScaler for feature scaling
from sklearn.linear_model import LogisticRegression  # Import LogisticRegression classifier
from sklearn.ensemble import RandomForestClassifier  # Import RandomForestClassifier
from sklearn.svm import SVC  # Import Support Vector Machines (SVM) classifier
from sklearn.metrics import accuracy_score, precision_score, recall_score, f1_score, roc_auc_score  # Import evaluation metrics
```

Figure 7.1 Code snippet to import libraries.

```
# Load the Pima Indians Diabetes dataset
data = pd.read_csv("/content/diabetes.csv")  # Read the dataset using pandas' read_csv function
```

Figure 7.2 Code snippet to load the diabetes dataset.

and machine learning. Data manipulation is handled by the imported pandas library, while numerical operations are handled by the imported numpy library. In order to divide the data into a training set and a testing set, the train_test_split function, which is located in the sklearn.model_selection import, is used. In order to scale features, the StandardScaler class included in the sklearn.preprocessing package is imported. For the purpose of utilizing a variety of classification strategies, the LogisticRegression, RandomForestClassifier, & SVC classes are imported via the appropriate modules within sklearn. For the purpose of model evaluation, evaluation metrics such as accuracy_score, precision_score, recall_score, f1_score, and roc_auc_score are imported from sklearn.metrics. These lines of code lay the groundwork for the functionality and tools that will be required for the upcoming data analysis and tasks related to machine learning.

The above line as in Figure 7.2 reads the dataset that is included in a CSV file by utilizing the read_csv function that is located in the pandas library. The file location where the dataset may be found is "/content/diabetes.csv," which is the name that has been given to the CSV file that is being used. The file is read using the read_csv function, which then returns a DataFrame. This DataFrame is then assigned to a value known as data.

When these lines of code are executed, the dataset titled "Pima Indians Diabetes" is loaded into storage as a pandas DataFrame, and then it is allocated to the variable titled "data" for the purposes of further investigation and manipulation.

The lines of code that are provided in Figure 7.3 involve segmenting the database into features and target factors, as well as segmenting the data even further into testing and training sets. The "Outcome" column, which originally represented the characteristics, is removed from the initial data set

```
# Split the dataset into features (X) and target variable (y)
X = data.drop("Outcome", axis=1) # Features: drop the "Outcome" column
y = data["Outcome"] # Target variable: select the "Outcome" column

# Split the data into training and testing sets
X_train, X_test, y_train, y_test = train_test_split(X, y, test_size=0.2, random_state=42) # Split the data into training and testing sets
```

Figure 7.3 Code snippet to split the dataset.

```
# Perform feature scaling
scaler = StandardScaler()  # Create a StandardScaler object
X_train_scaled = scaler.fit_transform(X_train)  # Scale the training features
X_test_scaled = scaler.transform(X_test)  # Scale the testing features
```

Figure 7.4 Code snippet for feature scaling.

in order to make room for the X DataFrame. After choosing the "Outcome" item in the dataset, which stands in for the target variable, the y Series is finally ready to be generated. After that, the train_test_split procedure is called to separate the features (X) and the variable of interest (y) to separate sets for training and testing. The test_size=0.2 option instructs the model to reserve 20% of the data for the testing phase, while devoting the remaining 80% of the data to the learning phase. The exactness of the split may be guaranteed thanks to the random_state=42 argument.

Scaling of features is accomplished using the lines of code provided in Figure 7.4, by utilizing the StandardScaler class found in the sklearn. preprocessing package. In order to calculate the average and standard deviation of each feature based on the training data, a StandardScaler object with the name scaler is first constructed. This feature scaling step helps machine learning models that use these characteristics perform better and be easier to interpret.

7.4 MODEL EVALUATION AND TRAINING

Logistic Regression, Random Forest, and Support Vector Machines (SVM) are the three models of machine learning that can be trained and evaluated with the code that is provided. Utilizing the scaled training variables (X_train_scaled) and the matching target variable (y_train), the logistic regression algorithm is developed and trained. Following this step, predictions are performed using the trained Logistic Regression model on the scaled testing characteristics (X_test_scaled), and the values of the predictions are saved in the y_pred_logreg variable. In a comparable manner, the Random Forest approach and then the SVM model are both constructed, trained, and utilized for predictive purposes. The values that are predicted by Random Forest and SVM are each saved in their own separate variable known as y_pred_rf and y_pred_svm. These trained models can be assessed further using suitable metrics in order to measure how well they perform in terms of predicting the variable of interest. Refer to Figure 7.5 for the code snippet.

```
# Model Training and Evaluation

# Logistic Regression
logreg = LogisticRegression()  # Create a logistic regression classifier
logreg.fit(X_train_scaled, y_train)  # Train the logistic regression model
y_pred_logreg = logreg.predict(X_test_scaled)  # Make predictions using the logistic regression model

# Random Forest
rf_classifier = RandomForestClassifier()  # Create a Random Forest classifier
rf_classifier.fit(X_train_scaled, y_train)  # Train the Random Forest model
y_pred_rf = rf_classifier.predict(X_test_scaled)  # Make predictions using the Random Forest model

# Support Vector Machines (SVM)
svm_classifier = SVC()  # Create an SVM classifier
svm_classifier.fit(X_train_scaled, y_train)  # Train the SVM model
y_pred_svm = svm_classifier.predict(X_test_scaled)  # Make predictions using the SVM model
```

Figure 7.5 Code snippet for model training.

```
# Evaluate performance

# Logistic Regression
accuracy_logreg = accuracy_score(y_test, y_pred_logreg)  # Calculate accuracy for logistic regression
precision_logreg = precision_score(y_test, y_pred_logreg)  # Calculate precision for logistic regression
recall_logreg = recall_score(y_test, y_pred_logreg)  # Calculate recall for logistic regression
f1_logreg = f1_score(y_test, y_pred_logreg)  # Calculate F1 score for logistic regression
roc_auc_logreg = roc_auc_score(y_test, y_pred_logreg)  # Calculate ROC AUC score for logistic regression

# Random Forest
accuracy_rf = accuracy_score(y_test, y_pred_rf)  # Calculate accuracy for Random Forest
precision_rf = precision_score(y_test, y_pred_rf)  # Calculate precision for Random Forest
recall_rf = recall_score(y_test, y_pred_rf)  # Calculate recall for Random Forest
f1_rf = f1_score(y_test, y_pred_rf)  # Calculate F1 score for Random Forest
roc_auc_rf = roc_auc_score(y_test, y_pred_rf)  # Calculate ROC AUC score for Random Forest

# Support Vector Machines (SVM)
accuracy_svm = accuracy_score(y_test, y_pred_svm)  # Calculate accuracy for SVM
precision_svm = precision_score(y_test, y_pred_svm)  # Calculate precision for SVM
recall_svm = recall_score(y_test, y_pred_svm)  # Calculate recall for SVM
f1_svm = f1_score(y_test, y_pred_svm)  # Calculate F1 score for SVM
roc_auc_svm = roc_auc_score(y_test, y_pred_svm)  # Calculate ROC AUC score for SVM
```

Figure 7.6 Code snippet for model evaluation.

Evaluation metrics for the machine learning models are computed using the code that is provided in Figure 7.6, and these metrics are stored. Metrics such as accuracy, precision, recall, F1 score, and ROC AUC score are derived for each model (Logistic Regression, Random Forest, and SVM) through the comparison of the true target values (y_test) and the predicted values (y_pred) produced by each corresponding model. This is done by comparing the true target values to the predicted values. These metrics offer insights into the capacity of each model to perform and make predictions based on the test data.

We print all the four metrics calculated for each of three chosen models using the print() function and the variables in which the metrics are stored. Refer to Figure 7.7 for the code snippet of the same.

When these lines of code as provided in Figure 7.8 are executed, a bar plot as seen in Figure 7.9 will be produced in order to illustrate and compare the outcomes and metrics of all three trained models. The plot offers a graphical representation of a comparison of the performance of the models on the metrics that are examined.

7.5 CONCLUSION

In this chapter, we made our first foray into the world of model evaluation and performance metrics while making predictions about diabetes using machine learning strategies. Beyond just accuracy, we now have a comprehensive grasp of model evaluation due to the introduction of a variety of evaluation metrics, including accuracy, precision, recall, F1 score, and ROC

```
# Print performance metrics for Logistic Regression
print("Logistic Regression:")
print("Accuracy:", accuracy_logreg)
print("Precision:", precision_logreg)
print("Recall:", recall_logreg)
print("F1 Score:", f1_logreg)
print("ROC AUC:", roc_auc_logreg)
print()

# Print performance metrics for Random Forest
print("Random Forest:")
print("Accuracy:", accuracy_rf)
print("Precision:", precision_rf)
print("Recall:", recall_rf)
print("F1 Score:", f1_rf)
print("ROC AUC:", roc_auc_rf)
print()

# Print performance metrics for Support Vector Machines
print("Support Vector Machines:")
print("Accuracy:", accuracy_svm)
print("Precision:", precision_svm)
print("Recall:", recall_svm)
print("F1 Score:", f1_svm)
print("ROC AUC:", roc_auc_svm)

Logistic Regression:
Accuracy: 0.7532467532467533
Precision: 0.6491228070175439
Recall: 0.6727272727272727
F1 Score: 0.6607142857142858
ROC AUC: 0.7353535353535354

Random Forest:
Accuracy: 0.7337662337662337
Precision: 0.6129032258064516
Recall: 0.6909090909090909
F1 Score: 0.6495726495726496
ROC AUC: 0.7242424242424242

Support Vector Machines:
Accuracy: 0.7337662337662337
Precision: 0.6458333333333334
Recall: 0.5636363636363636
F1 Score: 0.6019417475728155
ROC AUC: 0.6959595959595959
```

Figure 7.7 Code snippet to print performance metrics.

```
import matplotlib.pyplot as plt

# Create a dictionary to store the performance metrics for each model
metrics = {
    'Logistic Regression': [accuracy_logreg, precision_logreg, recall_logreg, f1_logreg, roc_auc_logreg],
    'Random Forest': [accuracy_rf, precision_rf, recall_rf, f1_rf, roc_auc_rf],
    'Support Vector Machines': [accuracy_svm, precision_svm, recall_svm, f1_svm, roc_auc_svm]
}

# Create a dataframe from the metrics dictionary
metrics_df = pd.DataFrame(metrics, index=['Accuracy', 'Precision', 'Recall', 'F1 Score', 'ROC AUC'])

# Plot the performance metrics
metrics_df.plot(kind='bar', figsize=(10, 6))
plt.title('Performance Metrics Comparison')
plt.xlabel('Metrics')
plt.ylabel('Score')
plt.xticks(rotation=45)
plt.legend(bbox_to_anchor=(1.05, 1), loc='upper left')
plt.tight_layout()
plt.show()
```

Figure 7.8 Performance metric comparison code snippet.

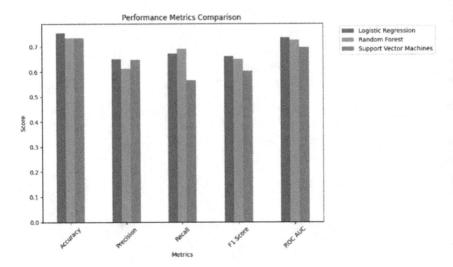

Figure 7.9 Performance metric comparison.

AUC score. The readers would have obtained knowledge about developing models, conducting feature scaling, and accurately evaluating model performance through the use of three different machine learning models on the Pima Indians Diabetes dataset.

7.6 FURTHER LEARNING

The Diabetes Dataset from the Pima Indians presents a considerable amount of promise for future research and technological breakthroughs in the field of diabetes forecasting. In terms of the engineering of features and the selection of the most important ones, additional research can be carried out to discover additional pertinent aspects that are unique to diabetes, as well as more sophisticated methods to either derive new features or choose the most important ones. In addition, the dataset may be put through more advanced machine learning procedures, such as the application of deep learning models, such as convolutional neural networks (CNNs) or recurrent neural networks (RNNs), which are able to identify subtle patterns and correlations hidden within the data.

SUGGESTED READINGS

Erickson, B.J. and Kitamura, F., 2021. Magician's corner: 9. Performance metrics for machine learning models. *Radiology: Artificial Intelligence*, 3(3), e200126.

Fabris, F., Doherty, A., Palmer, D., de Magalhaes, J.P. and Freitas, A.A., 2018. A new approach for interpreting random forest models and its application to the biology of ageing. *Bioinformatics*, *34*(14), pp.2449–2456.

O'Connell, A.A., 2006. *Logistic Regression Models for Ordinal Response Variables* (Vol. 146). Sage.

Sahoo, K.S., Tripathy, B.K., Naik, K., Ramasubbareddy, S., Balusamy, B., Khari, M. and Burgos, D., 2020. An evolutionary SVM model for DDOS attack detection in software defined networks. *IEEE Access*, *8*, pp.132502–132513.

Chapter 8

Parkinson's disease detection

An overview with feature engineering and outlier analysis

LEARNING OBJECTIVES

After reading this chapter, the reader shall be able to:

- Acquire the knowledge construct models to predict Parkinson's disease.
- Gain information regarding feature engineering, outlier analysis, model training, evaluation, and comparison.

8.1 INTRODUCTION

In this chapter, we will investigate how machine learning techniques can be applied to the diagnosis of Parkinson's disease. Readers can extract the dataset from the following link: www.kaggle.com/datasets/debasisdotcom/parkinson-disease-detection. The neuro degenerative condition known as Parkinson's disease is characterized by its effect on motor functioning. We are able to construct models that can predict the existence or absence of Parkinson's disease by making use of techniques that are associated with machine learning. These models examine a number of variables retrieved from patient data. Readers will be given an overview of the Parkinson Detection dataset as well as information regarding feature engineering, outlier analysis, model training, evaluation, and comparison throughout the course of this chapter.

8.2 IMPORTING LIBRARIES AND DATASET

Importing the necessary libraries for data manipulation, visualization, and machine learning is the first step (see Figure 8.1). For the purpose of data processing, the matplotlib and pandas libraries are loaded as pd. When attempting to visualize data, pyplot is notated as plt, and when attempting to enhance visualizations, seaborn is denoted as sns. We also import several modules from the sklearn library. These modules include train_test_split

DOI: 10.1201/9781032676685-9

```
import pandas as pd  # Importing the pandas library for data manipulation
import matplotlib.pyplot as plt  # Importing the matplotlib library for data visualization
import seaborn as sns  # Importing the seaborn library for enhanced visualizations
from sklearn.model_selection import train_test_split  # Importing train_test_split function for data splitting
from sklearn.preprocessing import StandardScaler, PolynomialFeatures  # Importing StandardScaler and PolynomialFeatures for data preprocessing
from sklearn.ensemble import IsolationForest  # Importing IsolationForest for outlier analysis
from sklearn.discriminant_analysis import LinearDiscriminantAnalysis  # Importing LinearDiscriminantAnalysis for LDA
from sklearn.linear_model import LinearRegression  # Importing LinearRegression for linear regression
from sklearn.tree import DecisionTreeClassifier  # Importing DecisionTreeClassifier for decision tree classification
from sklearn.metrics import accuracy_score  # Importing accuracy_score for evaluating model performance
```

Figure 8.1 Importing the needed libraries.

```
# Load the dataset
data = pd.read_csv('/content/parkinsons.csv')
```

```
data.head(2)
```

	name	MDVP:Fo(Hz)	MDVP:Fhi(Hz)	MDVP:Flo(Hz)	MDVP:Jitter(%)	MDVP:Jitter(Abs)	MDVP:RAP
0	phon_R01_S01_1	119.992	157.302	74.997	0.00784	0.00007	0.00370
1	phon_R01_S01_2	122.400	148.650	113.819	0.00968	0.00008	0.00465

2 rows × 24 columns

Figure 8.2 Code snippet to load the dataset.

for the purpose of data splitting, StandardScaler and PolynomialFeatures for the purpose of data preprocessing, IsolationForest for the purpose of outlier analysis, LinearDiscriminantAnalysis for the purpose of performing LDA, LinearRegression for the purpose of linear regression, and DecisionTreeClassifier for the purpose of decision tree classification. In addition, we bring in the accuracy_score variable so that we may assess how well our models are performing.

Finally we use the pd.read_csv function to load the dataset and we can see the first two rows from the dataset using the head(2) function as given in Figure 8.2.

8.3 DATA PRE-PROCESSING

8.3.1 Outlier detection and analysis

Outliers are data points that significantly deviate from the general pattern or distribution of the dataset. They are observations that are unusually distant from other observations and can have a substantial impact on the analysis and modeling process. Outliers can occur due to various reasons such as measurement errors, data entry mistakes, experimental anomalies, or genuine extreme values. Identifying and handling outliers is an essential step in data preprocessing as they can distort statistical analyses, affect the accuracy of machine learning models, and lead to misleading insights.

The number of rows and columns contained in the dataset is indicated by the "shape" of the data, which can be obtained by using the snippet of code known as data.shape as given in Figure 8.3. It supplies information regarding the parameters of the dataset. The features are extracted from the dataset using the code X = data.drop(["name," "status"], axis=1) as the separator. It does this by removing the columns "name" and "status" from the data in the first dataset, which results in the creation of a new DataFrame X. If you set the axis option to 1, it implies that the columns should be removed.

```
data.shape

(195, 24)


# Separate features and target variable
X = data.drop(['name', 'status'], axis=1)
y = data['status']
```

Figure 8.3 Code snippet for data shape.

When the line of code y = data["status"] is executed, the value of the target variable "status" is transferred to the variable y. It generates a new Series y using the values taken from the original dataset's "status" column and populating it with those values. The number of rows and columns contained within the features can be determined by using the code X.shape, which returns the shape of the features contained within DataFrame X. It offers details regarding the extent to which the feature set can be utilized.

In order to better illustrate the outcomes of the outlier detection, we generate a scatter plot with the help of matplotlib.pyplot and seaborn. The "MDVP:Fo(Hz)" feature is plotted along the y-axis, while the sample index is plotted along the x-axis. The hue parameter is used to color-code the outliers, so that the outliers are represented by a color that is distinct from the inliers' color representation. Refer to Figure 8.4. This gives us the ability to visually recognize the occurrences that are considered to be outliers based on where they are located in the scatter plot. (Note that while we chose the column MDVP:Fo(Hz) at random, this does not indicate that it is the sole column that contains outliers.)

We utilize an unsupervised learning approach called IsolationForest as represented in Figure 8.5 to find outliers in the dataset. This algorithm discovers anomalies by separating instances of the dataset and looking for patterns that do not fit the norm. We start a new instance of IsolationForest with a contamination parameter of 0.05, which indicates that we anticipate that around 5% of the data will be abnormal. After that, in order to understand the fundamental structure of the data, we apply the outlier detector to the feature matrix X and run the fitting process. Next, we apply the trained outlier detector to the dataset in order to forecast the outliers using the predict() method that is attached to X. A label of -1 is given to outliers by the predict() method, while a label of 1 is given to inliers. By selecting only the inlier occurrences for which the projected label is 1, we are able to generate a new subset of the feature matrix known as X_no_outliers. In a similar

```
# Visualize Outlier Detection
plt.figure(figsize=(8, 6))
sns.scatterplot(x=X.index, y=X['MDVP:Fo(Hz)'], hue=outliers, palette='Set1')
plt.xlabel('Sample Index')
plt.ylabel('MDVP:Fo(Hz)')
plt.title('Outlier Detection: MDVP:Fo(Hz)')
plt.show()
```

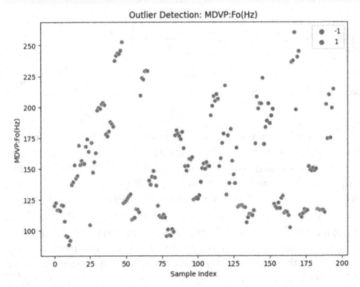

Figure 8.4 Outlier detection.

manner, we generate a comparable subset of the target variable called y_no_outliers by removing the outliers from the data.

8.3.2 The train-test split

For the function derived from sklearn.model_selection called train_test_split, we make use of the attributes X_no_outliers and the desired variable y_no_outliers, both composed of the filtered data that do not contain outliers. The test_size argument in Figure 8.6 allows the user to specify the percentage of the data used for testing, and the random_state parameter ensures that the split can be reproduced.

8.3.3 Scaling features

StandardScaler from the sklearn.preprocessing library as in Figure 8.7 is used to perform the scaling of the features. Scaling the training features

```
# Outlier Analysis
outlier_detector = IsolationForest(contamination=0.05)  # Creating an Isolation Forest outlier detector
outlier_detector.fit(X)  # Fitting the outlier detector on the features
outliers = outlier_detector.predict(X)  # Predicting outliers in the features
X_no_outliers= X[outliers == 1]  # Keeping only the non-outlier samples
y_no_outliers = y[outliers == 1]  # Keeping only the corresponding target variable

/usr/local/lib/python3.10/dist-packages/sklearn/base.py:439: UserWarning: X does not have valid feature names, but IsolationForest was fitted with feature names
  warnings.warn(

X_no_outliers.shape #outliers removed

(185, 22)
```

Figure 8.5 Outlier analysis.

```
# Split the data into training and testing sets
X_train, X_test, y_train, y_test = train_test_split(X_no_outliers, y_no_outliers, test_size=0.2, random_state=42)
```

Figure 8.6 Splitting the data.

```
# Perform feature scaling
scaler = StandardScaler()
X_train_scaled = scaler.fit_transform(X_train)
X_test_scaled = scaler.transform(X_test)
```

Figure 8.7 Code snippet to perform feature scaling.

(X_train) and the testing features (X_test) requires the StandardScaler to be instantiated as scaler so that it may be used. When the features are scaled, this guarantees that they are all on the same scale and prohibits any one feature from taking control of the learning algorithm.

8.3.4 Polynomial feature engineering

We will use polynomial feature engineering so that we can better understand the intricate connections between the features. Using this method, polynomial combinations of the initial characteristics are generated, which results in the creation of additional interaction terms. We will be able to more accurately describe non-linear relationships and maybe improve the performance of the model if we make use of higher-order terms. In this section, examples of code will be provided so as to explain the notion of polynomial feature engineering.

Following the scaling of the features, polynomial feature engineering is carried out (refer to Figure 8.8) with the help of the sklearn.preprocessing class PolynomialFeatures. In this particular instance, the degree of the polynomial is set to 2, denoted by the notation degree = 2. In order to convert the scaled training features (X_train_scaled) and testing features (X_test_scaled) into polynomial features, the PolynomialFeatures class is instantiated as the variable poly. This procedure creates new features by combining the existing features to the specified degree, which may then be used to build new features.

The modified features generated as a result, are saved in X_train_poly for the training data and X_test_poly for the testing data. These polynomial features capture non-linear correlations between the original data, allowing the models to learn more complicated patterns. This is made possible by the fact that the models are able to learn the patterns.

```
# Apply polynomial feature engineering
poly = PolynomialFeatures(degree=2)
X_train_poly = poly.fit_transform(X_train_scaled)
X_test_poly = poly.transform(X_test_scaled)
```

Figure 8.8 Code snippet for polynomial feature engineering.

8.4 MODEL TRAINING AND EVALUATION

In this section, we will train three distinct machine learning models: the Linear Discriminant Analysis (LDA), the Linear Regression, and the Decision Tree Classifier and then compare their performance. The training data will be used to fit each model, and the test data will be used to evaluate the models. In order to evaluate the efficacy of each model in predicting Parkinson's disease, we will compute the accuracy. The code snippet of this is provided in Figure 8.9.

This snippet of code as seen in Figure 8.10 generates a radar plot, which allows one to examine and evaluate the degrees of accuracy achieved by each of the three models. On the radar plot, each model is denoted by a vertex, and the distance of that vertex from the plot's center serves as an indicator of how accurate the model is. The greater the distance, the more accurate the measurement will be. The radar map makes it possible to conduct a rapid visual assessment of the accuracies of several different models. Adjusting the graph's size, line design, colors, and any other visual features to fit your tastes is one way you can personalize the plot.

8.5 FURTHER LEARNING

Future research and development could go in many different directions. To begin, we can investigate additional feature engineering strategies to further improve the performance of the model. Some of these techniques include feature selection and dimensionality reduction. In addition to this, we can experiment with a variety of machine learning algorithms and ensemble methods to determine whether any of them can produce superior results. In addition, the collection of additional data and the expansion of the dataset can result in models that are more resilient and generalizable. In conclusion, completing a more in-depth research and investigation into the characteristics that contribute the most to the prediction might provide significant insights for medical professionals who are working in the field. One may continue to refine and increase the accuracy and reliability of the Parkinson's disease detection that we have achieved via the use of machine learning by putting into practice and experimenting with a variety of methodologies and models.

8.6 CONCLUSION

The purpose of this chapter is to provide an overview of a machine learning experiment that makes use of the Parkinson Detection dataset. Following the completion of an outlier analysis and feature engineering by the use of polynomial transformation, the dataset is subjected to further processing. The preprocessed data are utilized in the application of three different

```
# Linear Discriminant Analysis (LDA)
lda = LinearDiscriminantAnalysis()   # Creating an LDA classifier
lda.fit(X_train_scaled, y_train)   # Fitting the LDA classifier on the training data
y_pred_lda = lda.predict(X_test_scaled)   # Making predictions using the LDA classifier
accuracy_lda = accuracy_score(y_test, y_pred_lda)   # Calculating accuracy of LDA predictions
print("LDA Accuracy:", accuracy_lda)

# Linear Regression
linear_reg = LinearRegression()   # Creating a Linear Regression model
linear_reg.fit(X_train_scaled, y_train)   # Fitting the Linear Regression model on the training data
y_pred_linear = linear_reg.predict(X_test_scaled)   # Making predictions using the Linear Regression model
y_pred_linear = [1 if val >= 0.5 else 0 for val in y_pred_linear]   # Converting predictions to binary values
accuracy_linear = accuracy_score(y_test, y_pred_linear)   # Calculating accuracy of Linear Regression predictions
print("Linear Regression Accuracy:", accuracy_linear)

# Decision Tree Classifier
dt_classifier = DecisionTreeClassifier()   # Creating a Decision Tree Classifier
dt_classifier.fit(X_train_poly, y_train)   # Fitting the Decision Tree Classifier on the polynomial features
y_pred_dt = dt_classifier.predict(X_test_poly)   # Making predictions using the Decision Tree Classifier
accuracy_dt = accuracy_score(y_test, y_pred_dt)   # Calculating accuracy of Decision Tree predictions
print("Decision Tree Accuracy:", accuracy_dt)

LDA Accuracy: 0.8918918918918919
Linear Regression Accuracy: 0.8918918918918919
Decision Tree Accuracy: 0.8648648648648649
```

Figure 8.9 Code snippet for training the machine learning models.

```
import numpy as np
import matplotlib.pyplot as plt
# Create a list of model names and their corresponding accuracies
models = ['LDA', 'Linear Regression', 'Decision Tree']
accuracies = [accuracy_lda, accuracy_linear, accuracy_dt]
# Calculate the number of models
num_models = len(models)
# Create an array of angles for the radar plot
angles = np.linspace(0, 2 * np.pi, num_models, endpoint=False).tolist()
angles += angles[:1]  # Close the plot by repeating the first angle
# Convert the accuracies to a circular format
circular_accuracies = accuracies + [accuracies[0]]
# Create a figure and axis for the radar plot
fig, ax = plt.subplots(figsize=(5, 5), subplot_kw={'polar': True})
# Plot the radar plot
ax.plot(angles, circular_accuracies, 'o-', linewidth=2)
# Set the labels for each axis
ax.set_xticks(angles[:-1])
ax.set_xticklabels(models)
# Set the y-axis limit based on the maximum accuracy
max_accuracy = max(accuracies)
ax.set_ylim(0, max_accuracy + 0.1)
# Set the title and gridlines
ax.set_title('Accuracy Comparison', pad=20)
ax.grid(True)
# Display the radar plot
plt.show()
```

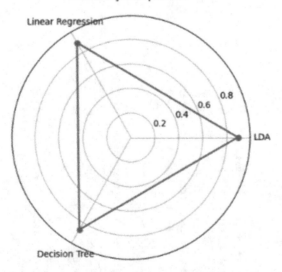

Figure 8.10 Accuracy comparison.

machine learning models viz. Linear Discriminant Analysis (LDA), Linear Regression, and Decision Tree Classification. After calculating and comparing the accuracy scores of various models, we arrived at a conclusion. The accuracy of LDA is estimated as 89.18%, while the accuracy of Linear Regression is also the same 89.18% as the LDA, whereas the accuracy of the Decision Tree Classifier is found to be 86.48%. Based on these findings, we conclude that the LDA as well as the Linear Regression model perform significantly better than the other model i.e., Decision Tree Classifier in predicting the presence of Parkinson's disease. On the other hand, additional research and testing could be required in order to ascertain which model is the best appropriate for this particular dataset.

SUGGESTED READINGS

Aalen, O.O., 1989. A linear regression model for the analysis of life times. *Statistics in Medicine*, 8(8), pp.907–925.

Dixon, W.J., 1953. Processing data for outliers. *Biometrics*, 9(1), pp.74–89.

Gaidel, A.V., 2018, September. Polynomial feature engineering for classification of textural images. *Journal of Physics: Conference Series*, 1096(1), 012027.

Izenman, A.J. and Izenman, A.J., 2008. Linear discriminant analysis. In *Modern Multivariate Statistical Techniques: Regression, Classification, and Manifold Learning* (pp.237–280). Springer.

Priyam, A., Abhijeeta, G.R., Rathee, A. and Srivastava, S., 2013. Comparative analysis of decision tree classification algorithms. *International Journal of Current Engineering and Technology*, 3(2), pp.334–337.

Chapter 9

Sonar mines vs. rock prediction using ensemble learning

LEARNING OBJECTIVES

By the end of this chapter, the reader shall be able to:

- Acquire knowledge about ensemble learning and its significance.
- Gain insights regarding reliable and accurate predictions with ensemble technique.

9.1 INTRODUCTION

In this chapter, we provide the readers with a concise introduction to ensemble learning and demonstrate how significantly it enhances the performance of our models. We plan to use the data that we have obtained from Kaggle which can be obtained from the following link: www.kaggle. com/datasets/mattcarter865/mines-vs-rocks?select=sonar.all-data.csv to make an educated guess as to whether the submarine is detecting a stone or a mine. The forecasts of a number of different machine learning models can be merged using the ensemble technique, which then provides us with reliable and accurate predictions. In addition to this, we have harnessed the power of oneAPI in order to improve the functionality of our models as well as their precision. In order to perfect our models, we make use of the oneDAL library provided by oneAPI.

9.2 IMPORTING LIBRARIES AND DATASET

First, we begin by importing all the necessary libraries that we would now need.

In order to work with the dataset and to manage it, we import the pandas library. Next, we import the train test split function in order to divide our data for the model into the testing set and the train set. We will be utilizing the Standard Scalar so that the features of the dataset may be standardized. These three models are obtained from the scikit-learn website and imported.

DOI: 10.1201/9781032676685-10

```
[1]: # Import necessary libraries
     import pandas as pd
     from sklearn.model_selection import train_test_split
     from sklearn.preprocessing import StandardScaler
     from sklearn.ensemble import RandomForestClassifier, VotingClassifier
     from sklearn.tree import DecisionTreeClassifier
     from sklearn.linear_model import LogisticRegression
     from sklearn.metrics import accuracy_score, classification_report
```

Figure 9.1 Importing the desired libraries.

```
# Read the "Sonar Mines vs Rocks" dataset
data = pd.read_csv("sonar.all-data.csv")
```

Figure 9.2 Loading the dataset.

To put the technique of ensemble learning into action, we need to import the votingclassifier. Importing the accuracy_score and classification_report helps us with both the results and the evaluation. See Figure 9.1.

Importing the csv file used for this project into the Pandas dataframe causes it to be saved in a variable that is simply named data. Refer to Figure 9.2 for the code snippet.

9.3 INITIAL EXPLORATION

For additional preprocessing in the subsequent sections, we need to further examine the dataset.

In order to examine the dataset, we make use of the .head() function, which provides us with the first five rows of the dataset. There are 61 columns and 5 rows in the dataset as seen from Figure 9.3. In the dataset, the Rock or Mine targets are located in the column labeled "R."

The presence of null values constitutes a possible risk that may result in a variety of complications during the modeling phase. To prevent this, we make use of the isnull().sum() as seen in Figure 9.4 that helps us determine the missing values from our dataset. Fortunately, none of those is seen in this data set.

9.4 DATA PRE-PROCESSING

Before feeding the data to our model, we first need to split our dataset into test set and train set.

[3]: data.head()

[3]:

	0.0200	0.0371	0.0428	0.0207	0.0954	0.0986	0.1539	0.1601	0.3109	0.2111	...	0.0027	0.0065	0.0159	0.0072	0.0167	0.0180	0.0084	0.0090	0.0032	R
0	0.0453	0.0523	0.0843	0.0689	0.1183	0.2583	0.2156	0.3481	0.3337	0.2872	...	0.0084	0.0089	0.0048	0.0094	0.0191	0.0140	0.0049	0.0052	0.0044	R
1	0.0262	0.0582	0.1099	0.1083	0.0974	0.2280	0.2431	0.3771	0.5598	0.6194	...	0.0232	0.0166	0.0095	0.0180	0.0244	0.0316	0.0164	0.0095	0.0078	R
2	0.0100	0.0171	0.0623	0.0205	0.0205	0.0368	0.1098	0.1276	0.0598	0.1264	...	0.0121	0.0036	0.0150	0.0085	0.0073	0.0050	0.0044	0.0040	0.0117	R
3	0.0762	0.0666	0.0481	0.0394	0.0590	0.0649	0.1209	0.2467	0.3564	0.4459	...	0.0031	0.0054	0.0105	0.0110	0.0015	0.0072	0.0048	0.0107	0.0094	R
4	0.0286	0.0453	0.0277	0.0174	0.0384	0.0990	0.1201	0.1833	0.2105	0.3039	...	0.0045	0.0014	0.0038	0.0013	0.0089	0.0057	0.0027	0.0051	0.0062	R

5 rows × 61 columns

Figure 9.3 Examining the dataset.

```
[4]: data.isnull().sum()

[4]: 0.0200     0
     0.0371     0
     0.0428     0
     0.0207     0
     0.0954     0
                ..
     0.0180     0
     0.0084     0
     0.0090     0
     0.0032     0
     R          0
     Length: 61, dtype: int64
```

Figure 9.4 Determining null values.

```
[6]: # Separate features (X) and labels (y) from the dataset
     X = data.drop("R", axis=1)
     y = data["R"]

[7]:
     # Split the data into training and testing sets
     X_train, X_test, y_train, y_test = train_test_split(X, y, test_size=0.2, random_state=42)
```

Figure 9.5 Dataset splitting.

```
[8]: # Standardize the feature data to have zero mean and unit variance
     scaler = StandardScaler()
     X_train_scaled = scaler.fit_transform(X_train)
     X_test_scaled = scaler.transform(X_test)
```

Figure 9.6 Dataset standardization.

In the first step as denoted in Figure 9.5, we establish two variables, which we will refer to as X and Y. In X, we will store the features apart from the target variable, and in Y, we will save only the target variable. In this scenario, we are aiming for R. Then, in order to split the data, we make use of the train_test_split function, with the test size set at 20% and the training size set at 80%.

StandardScaler, as seen from Figure 9.6, is an application that is utilized in order to resize the distribution of values in such a way that the mean of the observed values is equal to 0 and the standard deviation is equal to 1. StandardScaler is an important approach that is mostly used as a preprocessing step before many different machine learning models in order to standardize the range of functionality of the input dataset. This is done in order to ensure that the models can make accurate comparisons between the datasets.

9.5 MODEL TRAINING

A Voting Classifier is a type of machine learning model that is trained on an ensemble of many models and then makes a prediction about an output (class) based on the models' highest likelihood of selecting that class as the output. It merely compiles the results of each classifier fed into the Voting Classifier and bases which is the fundamental principle or rule upon which the Voting Classifier makes its final decision. Refer to Figure 9.7 for the code snippet.

There are three separate classification models employed, and then a voting classifier as given in Figure 9.8 is used to integrate the predictions from all the models. The red colored pop-up message shows us the models are optimized with oneAPI, oneDAL library.

The three model instances are saved in the variable referred to as "models" as a list of tuples, each of which has a unique name for a classifier. Following this step, a voting classifier is developed in order to carry out majority voting based on projected class labels. The final step is fitting the test data, which has previously been scaled, to the voting classifier.

9.6 RESULT AND ANALYSIS

As the final step, we analyze and evaluate the voting classifier that is created.

The accuracy of the voting classifier's prediction is compared with the ground truth labels using "accuracy_score." A classification report is then generated which includes various different metrics to evaluate our model. The model performs with an accuracy of 73.8% (refer to Figure 9.9).

9.7 FURTHER LEARNING

In the future, we may delve further into ensemble learning by investigating other approaches for ensemble learning such as bagging, boosting, and stacking. It is important to practice hyperparameter adjustment in order to enhance model performance. Additionally, it is important to research approaches for improving model interpretability and managing imbalanced datasets. Conduct experiments with a variety of model selection procedures, such as soft voting, and investigate in advanced ways for combining models, such as stacking using meta-classifiers.

9.8 CONCLUSION

In this chapter, we have discussed the idea of ensemble learning and illustrated how to use the Voting Classifier to combine the predictions of three different types of models: logistic regression, decision trees, and random forests. With ensemble learning, we were able to capitalize on the many models' inherent

```
[9]: from sklearnex import patch_sklearn
     patch_sklearn()
     from sklearn.ensemble import VotingClassifier

     # Create instances of three classifiers: Random Forest, Decision Trees, and Logistic Regression
     random_forest = RandomForestClassifier(n_estimators=100, random_state=42)
     decision_tree = DecisionTreeClassifier(random_state=42)
     logistic_regression = LogisticRegression(random_state=42)

     # Store the classifiers in a list of tuples along with their names
     models = [("Random Forest", random_forest),
               ("Decision Tree", decision_tree),
               ("Logistic Regression", logistic_regression)]

     Intel(R) Extension for Scikit-learn* enabled (https://github.com/intel/scikit-learn-intelex)
```

Figure 9.7 Voting Classifier.

```
[10]: # Create the Voting Classifier to combine predictions from multiple models using majority voting
      voting_classifier = VotingClassifier(estimators=models, voting='hard')

      # Train the Voting Classifier on the scaled training data
      voting_classifier.fit(X_train_scaled, y_train)

      # Use the Voting Classifier to make predictions on the scaled test data
      y_pred = voting_classifier.predict(X_test_scaled)
```

Figure 9.8 To integrate predictions from all models.

```
[11]: # Evaluate the performance of the Voting Classifier
      accuracy = accuracy_score(y_test, y_pred)
      classification_rep = classification_report(y_test, y_pred)

      # Print the results
      print("Voting Classifier Results:")
      print("Accuracy:", accuracy)
      print("Classification Report:")
      print(classification_rep)

      Voting Classifier Results:
      Accuracy: 0.7380952380952381
      Classification Report:
                     precision    recall  f1-score   support

                 M       0.79      0.81      0.80        27
                 R       0.64      0.60      0.62        15

          accuracy                           0.74        42
         macro avg       0.71      0.71      0.71        42
      weighted avg       0.73      0.74      0.74        42
```

Figure 9.9 Voting Classifier performance evaluation.

advantages, which ultimately led to a more reliable and accurate categorization. We were able to have a better grasp of how ensemble learning can dramatically improve the performance and stability of machine learning models by using this approach. As we continue to work our way through this book, we will go deeper into more advanced principles and methods of machine learning, which will provide us with the ability to efficiently solve difficult problems that arise in the real world.

SUGGESTED READING

Karadeniz, T., Maraş, H.H, Tokdemir, G. and Ergezer, H., 2023, March 15. Two majority voting classifiers applied to heart disease prediction. *Applied Sciences*, 13(6), p.3767.

Chapter 10

Bankruptcy risk prediction

LEARNING OBJECTIVES

After reading this chapter, the reader shall be able to:

- Acquire the knowledge to develop a reliable machine learning model for financial purposes to determine the risk of bankrupt.
- Gain information regarding data pretreatment, data exploration, model construction as well as result analysis.

10.1 INTRODUCTION

The process of identifying failing companies using methods of machine learning is what we will be exploring in this chapter. The objective variable "Bankrupt" in our dataset "Bankruptcy_Detection" can be obtained from Kaggle by using the following link: www.kaggle.com/datasets/fede soriano/company-bankruptcy-prediction which indicates whether or not a company has filed for bankruptcy. This dataset provides essential financial indicators and ratios for a variety of enterprises. The objective of this project is to develop a reliable machine learning model with the capability of determining, on the basis of the financial characteristics of a business, whether or not that business is at risk of going bankrupt. In order to provide useful insights into this important financial application, we will take a methodical approach, which will include data pretreatment, data exploration, model construction, result analysis, and concluding remarks.

10.2 IMPORTING LIBRARIES AND DATASET

Initially to prepare the dataset for modeling, we need to perform some data preparation. During this stage, you will be responsible for resolving any missing numbers and addressing any data quality issues that may have arisen. Let us get started by loading the dataset, analyzing its structure, and

DOI: 10.1201/9781032676685-11

```
#importing required libraries
import pandas as pd
from sklearn.model_selection import train_test_split
from sklearn.preprocessing import StandardScaler
from sklearn.ensemble import RandomForestClassifier
from sklearn.svm import SVC
from sklearn.metrics import accuracy_score, classification_report
from imblearn.over_sampling import SMOTE
from imblearn.under_sampling import RandomUnderSampler
import matplotlib.pyplot as plt
import seaborn as sns
```

Figure 10.1 Importing the necessary libraries.

```
]
    # Load the "Bankruptcy_Detection" dataset
    data = pd.read_csv("/content/data.csv")
```

Figure 10.2 Code snippet to load the dataset.

managing the null values by populating them with the mean of each column. This will get us off to a good start.

We begin by importing the necessary library files as witnessed in Figure 10.1. Pandas is used for data handling, train_test_split is utilized for splitting the dataset, StandardScaler is utilized for feature scaling, RandomForestClassifier is utilized for the construction of the Random Forest model, accuracy_score and classification_report are utilized as model evaluation metrics, and SMOTE and RandomUnderSampler are utilized for the treatment of class imbalance.

We use pandas to read the "Bankruptcy_Detection" dataset from the csv file, and then we save it in a DataFrame that we've given the name data. Refer to Figure 10.2 for the code snippet.

10.3 DATA EXPLORATION AND PREPROCESSING

In this step, we are looking at the first five rows of our dataset to get an overview about the features present. It is clear that we have 5 rows and 96 columns as seen in Figure 10.3 with "Bankrupt?" as our target variable.

Next, we check for the null values in our dataset using the isnull().sum() function. We can see some features contain null values as in Figure 10.4.

`data.head()`

	Bankrupt?	ROA(C) before interest and depreciation before interest	ROA(A) before interest and % after tax	ROA(B) before interest and depreciation after tax	Operating Gross Margin	Realized Sales Gross Margin	Operating Profit Rate	Pre-tax net Interest Rate	After-tax net Interest Rate	Non-industry income and expenditure/revenue	...
0	1	0.370594	0.424389	0.405750	0.601457	0.601457	0.998969	0.796887	0.808809	0.302646	...
1	1	0.464291	0.538214	0.516730	0.610235	0.610235	0.998946	0.797380	0.809301	0.303556	...
2	1	0.426071	0.499019	0.472295	0.601450	0.601364	0.998857	0.796403	0.808388	0.302035	...
3	1	0.399844	0.451265	0.457733	0.583541	0.583541	0.998700	0.796967	0.808966	0.303350	...
4	1	0.465022	0.538432	0.522298	0.598783	0.598783	0.998973	0.797366	0.809304	0.303475	...

5 rows × 96 columns

Figure 10.3 Examining the dataset.

```
data.isnull().sum()
```

```
Bankrupt?                                                      0
 ROA(C) before interest and depreciation before interest       0
 ROA(A) before interest and % after tax                        0
 ROA(B) before interest and depreciation after tax             0
 Operating Gross Margin                                         0
                                                               ..
 Liability to Equity                                            1
 Degree of Financial Leverage (DFL)                             1
 Interest Coverage Ratio (Interest expense to EBIT)            1
 Net Income Flag                                                1
 Equity to Liability                                            1
Length: 96, dtype: int64
```

Figure 10.4 Checking null values.

```
# Fill null values with the mean of each column
data.fillna(data.mean(), inplace=True)
```

```
data.isnull().sum()
```

```
Bankrupt?                                                      0
 ROA(C) before interest and depreciation before interest       0
 ROA(A) before interest and % after tax                        0
 ROA(B) before interest and depreciation after tax             0
 Operating Gross Margin                                         0
                                                               ..
 Liability to Equity                                            0
 Degree of Financial Leverage (DFL)                             0
 Interest Coverage Ratio (Interest expense to EBIT)            0
 Net Income Flag                                                0
 Equity to Liability                                            0
Length: 96, dtype: int64
```

Figure 10.5 Filling the null values.

From the previous step, we have an idea about the data type present. We have to choose a suitable method to fill all the null values.

To fill the null values we use the mean method as depicted in Figure 10.5. Now it is evident that our data set does not contain any null values.

We divide the feature columns (X) and the target variable column ("Bankrupt?") and then store them, separately, in the variables X and y. After that, we use the train_test_split function that is included in the

```
# Separate features (X) and labels (y) from the dataset
X = data.drop("Bankrupt?", axis=1)
y = data["Bankrupt?"]
```

```
# Split the data into training and testing sets
X_train, X_test, y_train, y_test = train_test_split(X, y, test_size=0.2, random_state=42)
```

Figure 10.6 Feature separation and dataset splitting.

```
# Standardize the feature data to have zero mean and unit variance
scaler = StandardScaler()
X_train_scaled = scaler.fit_transform(X_train)
X_test_scaled = scaler.transform(X_test)
```

Figure 10.7 Feature data scaling.

scikit-learn package to divide the dataset into a training set and a testing set. The training set accounts for 80 percent of the total data, whereas the test set accounts for 20 percent. The random_state=42 parameter assures that the results may be reproduced accurately. Refer to Figure 10.6 for the code snippet.

In order to scale the feature data, an instance of StandardScaler is first created. Scaling guarantees that all features have comparable ranges and prevents features with bigger scales from taking control of the learning process. Scaling can also be used to describe the relationship between two variables. We start by fitting the scaler to the training data using fit_transform, and then we use the fitted scaler to transform both the training data and the testing data. Refer to Figure 10.7 for the code snippet.

In order to discover any potential class imbalances, we first visualize the distribution of the target variable "Bankrupt?" and then conduct an analysis of its class distribution. The illustration presented in Figure 10.8 makes it abundantly evident that there is an imbalance of classes (Japkowicz and Stephen, 2002).

To address the issue of class imbalance, an instance of SMOTE is created. SMOTE is able to generate synthetic samples for the minority class by interpolating new samples between the ones that already exist for the minority class. By resampling the training data with the fit_resample function, we are able to generate a version of the training data that is more

```
import matplotlib.pyplot as plt

# Visualize the distribution of the target variable "Bankrupt?"
plt.figure(figsize=(6, 4))
data["Bankrupt?"].value_counts().plot(kind="bar", color=["skyblue", "orange"])
plt.xlabel("Bankrupt?")
plt.ylabel("Count")
plt.title("Distribution of Bankrupt?")
plt.xticks([0, 1], ["Not Bankrupt", "Bankrupt"])
plt.show()
```

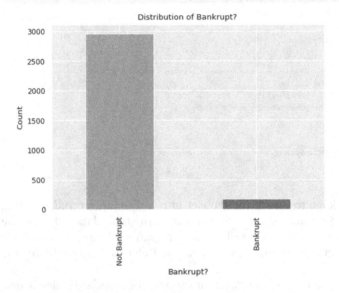

Figure 10.8 Class imbalances visualization.

evenly distributed with regard to the target variable. In order to tackle class imbalance in a more comprehensive manner, we first build an instance of the RandomUnderSampler. Random Under-Sampling is a technique that removes samples from the majority class in order to create a more even distribution across the classes. In order to produce the completed form of the balanced training data (X_train_balanced and y_train_balanced), we apply this method to the data that was already balanced during the training process. Refer to Figure 10.9 for the code snippet.

10.4 MODELING

We begin by generating a Random Forest Classifier with 100 trees (n_estimators=100) and setting the random seed to ensure reproducibility

```
# Handling class imbalance using SMOTE (Synthetic Minority Over-sampling Technique)
smote = SMOTE(random_state=42)
X_train_balanced, y_train_balanced = smote.fit_resample(X_train_scaled, y_train)


# Handling class imbalance using Random Under-Sampling
rus = RandomUnderSampler(random_state=42)
X_train_balanced, y_train_balanced = rus.fit_resample(X_train_balanced, y_train_balanced)
```

Figure 10.9 Addressing Class imbalance.

```
# Create a Random Forest Classifier
random_forest = RandomForestClassifier(n_estimators=100, random_state=42)

# Train the Random Forest Classifier on the balanced training data
random_forest.fit(X_train_balanced, y_train_balanced)

# Create an SVM classifier
svm_model = SVC(random_state=42)

# Train the SVM classifier on the balanced training data
svm_model.fit(X_train_balanced, y_train_balanced)
```

```
      ▼          SVC
SVC(random_state=42)
```

Figure 10.10 Classifier generation and training.

(random_state=42). The complete code snippet is provided in Figure 10.10. Next, we generate an SVM classifier with the name svm_model and train it on the balanced training data (X_train_balanced and y_train_balanced). Finally, we generate a final model. On the balanced training data (X_train_balanced and y_train_balanced), we train the Random Forest and the SVM model. To make a prediction about the target variable based on the scaled test data (X_test_scaled), we make use of the trained Random Forest and svm model.

To make a prediction about the target variable based on the scaled test data (X_test_scaled), we make use of the trained Random Forest and svm model. Using the ground truth labels from the test set (y_test) and the predicted

```
# Use the trained models to make predictions on the test data
y_pred_rf = random_forest.predict(X_test_scaled)
y_pred_svm = svm_model.predict(X_test_scaled)

# Evaluate the performance of the models
accuracy_rf = accuracy_score(y_test, y_pred_rf)
accuracy_svm = accuracy_score(y_test, y_pred_svm)

classification_rep_rf = classification_report(y_test, y_pred_rf)
classification_rep_svm = classification_report(y_test, y_pred_svm)
```

Figure 10.11 Predictions and Performance evaluation.

labels (y_pred), we calculate the accuracy of the model's predictions as seen from Figure 10.11. The next step is the generation of a comprehensive classification report, which evaluates the performance of the model by providing metrics such as precision, recall, F1-score, and support for each class.

10.5 RESULT AND ANALYSIS

The evaluation results, which include the report on the model's accuracy as well as a full classification of the data, are printed with the aid of the code given in Figure 10.12. Random forest outperforms SVM with an accuracy of around 91.69%.

To visualize the difference in accuracy between the two models, we generate a bar plot as shown in Figure 10.13 with matplotlib and use plt.bar as the plotting function. The accuracy values are displayed along the y-axis of the bar plot, while the model names are listed along the x-axis. The bar plot provides a visual comparison of the accuracy of the SVM classifier and the Random Forest classifier, which will assist us in determining whether the model performs better for the identification of bankruptcy on this dataset.

10.6 CONCLUSION

Our investigation on the possibility of bankruptcy utilizing machine learning seems fruitful. We begin the bankruptcy prediction procedure by first preprocessing the dataset, then visually representing the target variable distribution, and finally training Random Forest and SVM models. We made use of a variety of indicators to evaluate the performance of the models, which allow us to identify both their strengths and limitations. This project offers useful insights for the use of machine learning in bankruptcy risk assessment, thereby assisting financial professionals in making judgments that are more informed.

```
# Print the results
print("Random Forest Classifier Results:")
print("Accuracy:", accuracy_rf)
print("Classification Report:")
print(classification_rep_rf)

print("\nSVM Classifier Results:")
print("Accuracy:", accuracy_svm)
print("Classification Report:")
print(classification_rep_svm)
```

```
Random Forest Classifier Results:
Accuracy: 0.9169329073482428
Classification Report:
                precision    recall  f1-score   support

           0        0.96      0.95      0.96       592
           1        0.30      0.38      0.33        34

    accuracy                            0.92       626
   macro avg        0.63      0.66      0.64       626
weighted avg        0.93      0.92      0.92       626


SVM Classifier Results:
Accuracy: 0.8817891373801917
Classification Report:
                precision    recall  f1-score   support

           0        0.98      0.90      0.93       592
           1        0.26      0.65      0.37        34

    accuracy                            0.88       626
   macro avg        0.62      0.77      0.65       626
weighted avg        0.94      0.88      0.90       626
```

Figure 10.12 Results Evaluation.

10.7 FURTHER WORKS

In future works, we may investigate more complex machine learning models, such as neural networks or gradient boosting techniques, with the goal of significantly improving the accuracy of bankruptcy identification. In addition, the incorporation of alternative data sources, the incorporation

```
# Create a bar plot to compare the accuracy of Random Forest and SVM
accuracies = [accuracy_rf, accuracy_svm]
models = ['Random Forest', 'SVM']

plt.bar(models, accuracies, color=['skyblue', 'orange'])
plt.xlabel('Models')
plt.ylabel('Accuracy')
plt.title('Comparison of Accuracy: Random Forest vs. SVM')
plt.show()
```

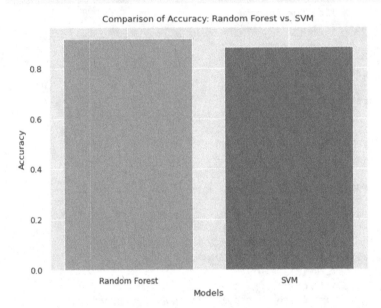

Figure 10.13 Accuracy comparison.

of time-series data, and the consideration of domain-specific financial characteristics could boost the performance of the model. In addition, the use of interpretability methodologies and the performance of feature importance analysis will provide insightful knowledge that will be helpful for financial professionals in their quest to comprehend the elements that influence bankruptcy predictions.

SUGGESTED READING

Japkowicz, N. and Stephen, S., 2002. The class imbalance problem: A systematic study. *Intelligent Data Analysis*, 6(5), pp.429–449.

Chapter 11

Hotel reservation prediction

LEARNING OBJECTIVES

After finishing this chapter, the reader shall be able to:

- Discover insights and construct predictive models by utilizing the power of exploratory data analysis and machine learning models.
- Build and analyze the prediction models.
- Efficiently plan hotel operations, revenue generation and enhance customer happiness based on the data-driven insights and precise predictions.

11.1 INTRODUCTION

In today's modern hospitality sector, it is absolutely essential to manage hotel reservations in an effective manner in order to provide excellent experiences for guests. Exploration and prediction code based on the "Hotel Reservation Dataset" from kaggle, www.kaggle.com/datasets/ahsan81/hotel-reservati ons-classification-dataset, provides a comprehensive solution to study and forecast booking results. This code gives data enthusiasts and hospitality professionals the ability to discover insights and construct predictive models by utilizing the power of exploratory data analysis (EDA), preprocessing, and machine learning models. The dataset is loaded and preprocessed as the first step in the algorithm, followed by the handling of missing values and the encoding of categorical variables. Following that, it demonstrates EDA by visualizing booking status distributions, correlations among attributes, and room type pricing. Building and analyzing prediction models through the use of logistic regression, decision trees, and random forests is the core functionality of the code. In addition to this, it uses techniques of oversampling in order to address the problem of class imbalance. The end goal is to create a comprehensive toolkit that can be utilized by anyone who has an interest in understanding the dynamics of hotel reservations and improving their ability to forecast future outcomes. People who use this code are

DOI: 10.1201/9781032676685-12

able to more effectively strategize hotel operations, maximize income, and improve customer happiness based on the data-driven insights and accurate predictions.

11.2 DATA PREPROCESSING

We start by importing the necessary libraries for the task, as shown in Figure 11.1. We import modules like pandas and numpy for handling data, and for data visualization, we import matplotlib and seaborn.

We then use the pandas library to load the csv data (Figure 11.2).

The head() function used gives us the first five rows of the datasets as seen in Figure 11.3.

info() gives us information about the structure of our dataset, whereas describe() gets a summary of the statistics of our dataset. Both are seen in Figures 11.4 and 11.5.

By exploring the dataset, it is evident that the Booking_ID column is not necessary for the predictions, so using the drop() function, we are able to drop the Booking_ID from the dataframe. Later, we used isnull().sum() to check for missing values, and it is evident that there are no missing values in our dataset. See Figure 11.6.

11.3 EXPLORATORY DATA ANALYSIS (EDA)

To check for class imbalance, we have used the countplot as depicted in Figure 11.7 to visualize the distribution of our target label, which is the booking status. It's clear that there is a variation between canceled and not-canceled classes. In later steps, we will take the necessary actions to overcome this issue.

```
# Import necessary libraries for data manipulation and visualization
import pandas as pd
import numpy as np
import matplotlib.pyplot as plt
import seaborn as sns
```

Figure 11.1 Code snippet to import libraries.

```
# Load the dataset from a CSV file and display initial information
data = pd.read_csv('/content/Hotel Reservations.csv')
```

Figure 11.2 To load the dataset.

```
data.head() # Display the first few rows of the dataset
```

	Booking_ID	no_of_adults	no_of_children	no_of_weekend_nights	no_of_week_nights	type_of_meal_plan	required_car_parking_space	room_type_reserved	lead_time	arrival_year	arrival_month	arrival_date	market_segment_type	repeate
0	INN00001	2	0	1	2	Meal Plan 1	0	Room_Type 1	224	2017	10	2	Offline	
1	INN00002	2	0	2	3	Not Selected	0	Room_Type 1	5	2018	11	6	Online	
2	INN00003	1	0	2	1	Meal Plan 1	0	Room_Type 1	1	2018	2	28	Online	
3	INN00004	2	0	0	2	Meal Plan 1	0	Room_Type 1	211	2018	5	20	Online	
4	INN00005	2	0	1	1	Not Selected	0	Room_Type 1	48	2018	4	11	Online	

Figure 11.3 Code snippet to look at the dataset.

```
data.info() # Get information about the dataset
data.describe()

<class 'pandas.core.frame.DataFrame'>
RangeIndex: 36275 entries, 0 to 36274
Data columns (total 19 columns):
 #   Column                                Non-Null Count   Dtype
---  ------                                --------------   -----
 0   Booking_ID                            36275 non-null   object
 1   no_of_adults                          36275 non-null   int64
 2   no_of_children                        36275 non-null   int64
 3   no_of_weekend_nights                  36275 non-null   int64
 4   no_of_week_nights                     36275 non-null   int64
 5   type_of_meal_plan                     36275 non-null   object
 6   required_car_parking_space            36275 non-null   int64
 7   room_type_reserved                    36275 non-null   object
 8   lead_time                             36275 non-null   int64
 9   arrival_year                          36275 non-null   int64
 10  arrival_month                         36275 non-null   int64
 11  arrival_date                          36275 non-null   int64
 12  market_segment_type                   36275 non-null   object
 13  repeated_guest                        36275 non-null   int64
 14  no_of_previous_cancellations          36275 non-null   int64
 15  no_of_previous_bookings_not_canceled  36275 non-null   int64
 16  avg_price_per_room                    36275 non-null   float64
 17  no_of_special_requests                36275 non-null   int64
 18  booking_status                        36275 non-null   object
dtypes: float64(1), int64(13), object(5)
memory usage: 5.3+ MB
```

Figure 11.4 Acquiring information from the dataset.

	no_of_adults	no_of_children	no_of_weekend_nights	no_of_week_nights	required_car_parking_space	
count	36275.000000	36275.000000	36275.000000	36275.000000	36275.000000	36
mean	1.844962	0.105279	0.810724	2.204300	0.030986	
std	0.518715	0.402648	0.870644	1.410905	0.173281	
min	0.000000	0.000000	0.000000	0.000000	0.000000	
25%	2.000000	0.000000	0.000000	1.000000	0.000000	
50%	2.000000	0.000000	1.000000	2.000000	0.000000	
75%	2.000000	0.000000	2.000000	3.000000	0.000000	
max	4.000000	10.000000	7.000000	17.000000	1.000000	

Figure 11.5 Acquiring description of the dataset.

```
data = data.drop('Booking_ID', axis=1)


# Check for missing values and remove rows with missing values
data.isnull().sum()  # Check count of missing values for each column
```

```
no_of_adults                              0
no_of_children                            0
no_of_weekend_nights                      0
no_of_week_nights                         0
type_of_meal_plan                         0
required_car_parking_space                0
room_type_reserved                        0
lead_time                                 0
arrival_year                              0
arrival_month                             0
arrival_date                              0
market_segment_type                       0
repeated_guest                            0
no_of_previous_cancellations              0
no_of_previous_bookings_not_canceled      0
avg_price_per_room                        0
no_of_special_requests                    0
booking_status                            0
dtype: int64
```

Figure 11.6 Exploring the dataset.

A simple correlation heatmap is created by following the code snippet as shown in Figure 11.8. We analyze and visualize the relationship between variables in the dataset as illustrated in Figure 11.9.

We then use boxplot as provided in Figure 11.10 to compare the room types based on the average price per room.

The particular code snippet shown in Figure 11.11 gives us the unique values present in the columns room_type_reserved,market_segment_type, type_of_meal_plan, and booking_status.

We then transform the data on the dataframe by mapping the unique strings we got from the previous stem to corresponding numeric values. See Figure 11.12 for the code snippet.

11.4 DATA SPLITTING

In this step, we prepare the features and targets. We initialize by separating the features and target and store them in a variable X and y separately.

```
# Visualize the distribution of booking statuses using a count plot
plt.figure(figsize=(8, 6))
sns.countplot(x='booking_status', data=data)
plt.title('Booking Status Distribution')
plt.show()
```

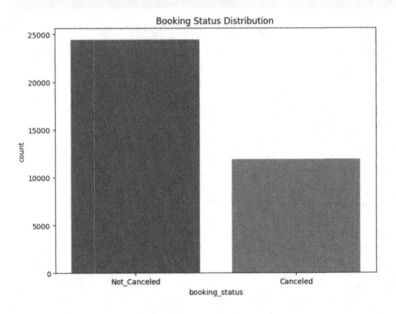

Figure 11.7 Visualization.

```
# Create a correlation heatmap to visualize relationships between numerical variables
corr_matrix = data.corr()
plt.figure(figsize=(12, 8))
sns.heatmap(corr_matrix, annot=True, cmap='coolwarm')
plt.title('Correlation Heatmap')
plt.show()
```

Figure 11.8 Code to Generate a Correlation heatmap.

Here, booking_status is our target variable. Then we split the data into training and testing sets for which we use the train_test_split() function. 20% of the data is used for testing, and 80% is used for training as evident from Figure 11.13.

As mentioned previously, we identify the class imbalance problem with our dataset. To handle this, we are oversampling the minority class. To upsample the minority class to that of the majority class, the resample() function is used. See Figure 11.14.

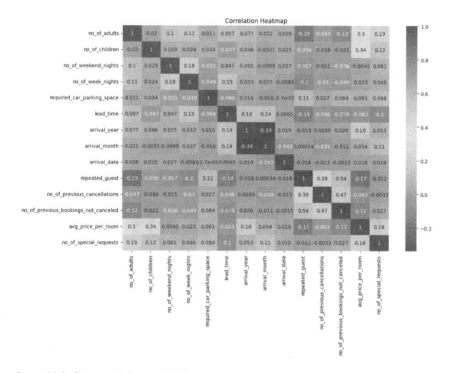

Figure 11.9 Generated Correlation heatmap.

11.5 MODEL BUILDING

For modeling, we use three different machine learning models: logistic regression, decision tree classification, and random forest classification, and import the necessary packages to initialize them as illustrated in Figure 11.15. All these models are trained with the resampled training data created in the previous step.

In the above code snippet of Figure 11.16, evaluate_model() function is used to generate the classification reports, calculate the accuracy for each model and store them.

11.6 MODEL EVALUATION AND COMPARISON

To understand more about the performance of each model we print the classification report and accuracy as in Figure 11.17.

In order to provide a graphical representation of the accuracy of the various models, we construct a bar chart as seen in Figure 11.18. The graphic sheds light on which model is more accurate by providing insights into which model performs better.

```
# Compare room types based on the average price per room using a box plot
plt.figure(figsize=(10, 6))
sns.boxplot(x='room_type_reserved', y='avg_price_per_room', data=data)
plt.title('Room Type vs. Average Price per Room')
plt.xticks(rotation=45)
plt.show()
```

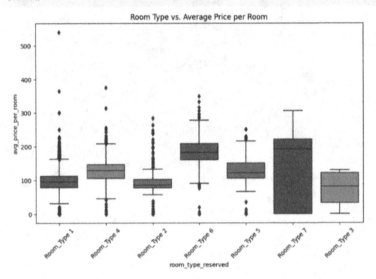

Figure 11.10 Boxplot for comparison.

```
#Finding Unique Values in various columns
data['room_type_reserved'].unique()
```

```
array(['Room_Type 1', 'Room_Type 4', 'Room_Type 2', 'Room_Type 6',
       'Room_Type 5', 'Room_Type 7', 'Room_Type 3'], dtype=object)
```

```
data['market_segment_type'].unique()
```

```
array(['Offline', 'Online', 'Corporate', 'Aviation', 'Complementary'],
      dtype=object)
```

```
data['type_of_meal_plan'] .unique()
```

```
array(['Meal Plan 1', 'Not Selected', 'Meal Plan 2', 'Meal Plan 3'],
      dtype=object)
```

Figure 11.11 Code snippet to find unique values.

```
#Mapping strings with Numbers
data['room_type_reserved'] = data['room_type_reserved'].map({'Room_Type 1': 1, 'Room_Type 2': 2, 'Room_Type 3': 3,
                                                             'Room_Type 4': 4, 'Room_Type 5': 5, 'Room_Type 6': 6, 'Room_Type 7': 7})

data['market_segment_type'] = data['market_segment_type'].map({'Offline': 0,'Online': 1,'Corporate': 2,'Aviation': 3,'Complementary': 4,})

data['booking_status'] = data['booking_status'].map({'Not_Canceled': 0, 'Canceled': 1})

data['type_of_meal_plan'] = data['type_of_meal_plan'].map({'Not Selected': 0, 'Meal Plan 1': 1, 'Meal Plan 2': 2, 'Meal Plan 3': 3})
```

Figure 11.12 Data transformation.

```
# Prepare features (X) and target (y)
X = data.drop(['booking_status'], axis=1)
y = data['booking_status']  # Use 'booking_status' as the target


# Split the data into training and testing sets
X_train, X_test, y_train, y_test = train_test_split(X, y, test_size=0.2, random_state=42)
```

Figure 11.13 Code snippet for data splitting.

```
# Handling class imbalance using oversampling (up-sampling the minority class)
from sklearn.utils import resample
X_train_resampled, y_train_resampled = resample(X_train[y_train == 1], y_train[y_train == 1],
                                                 n_samples=X_train[y_train == 0].shape[0],
                                                 replace=True, random_state=42)

X_train_resampled = pd.concat([X_train_resampled, X_train[y_train == 0]])
y_train_resampled = pd.concat([y_train_resampled, y_train[y_train == 0]])
```

Figure 11.14 Code snippet for class imbalance problem.

11.7 CONCLUSION

The power of data-driven decision-making in the hospitality industry has been brought to light as a result of the voyage via the "Hotel Reservation Dataset" exploration and prediction code. We were able to obtain priceless insights regarding booking patterns, client preferences, and market categories as a result of our painstaking dissection of the dataset. The utilization of exploratory data analysis (EDA) unearthed concealed patterns, which has assisted in our comprehension of the complex dynamic that exists between the many characteristics. We ensure that the dataset was ready for predictive modeling by performing meticulous preprocessing on it, which included managing cases of missing values and encoding categorical variables.

```
from sklearn.linear_model import LogisticRegression
from sklearn.tree import DecisionTreeClassifier
from sklearn.ensemble import RandomForestClassifier
# Initialize and train a Logistic Regression model
lr_model = LogisticRegression()
lr_model.fit(X_train_resampled, y_train_resampled)


# Initialize and train a Decision Tree Classifier model
dt_model = DecisionTreeClassifier()
dt_model.fit(X_train_resampled, y_train_resampled)


# Initialize and train a Random Forest Classifier model

rf_model = RandomForestClassifier()
rf_model.fit(X_train_resampled, y_train_resampled)
```

```
/usr/local/lib/python3.10/dist-packages/sklearn/linear_model/_logistic.py:458: ConvergenceWarning: lbfgs failed to converge (status=1):
STOP: TOTAL NO. of ITERATIONS REACHED LIMIT.

Increase the number of iterations (max_iter) or scale the data as shown in:
    https://scikit-learn.org/stable/modules/preprocessing.html
Please also refer to the documentation for alternative solver options:
    https://scikit-learn.org/stable/modules/linear_model.html#logistic-regression
  n_iter_i = _check_optimize_result(
```

```
• RandomForestClassifier
RandomForestClassifier()
```

Figure 11.15 Code snippet to import machine learning models.

```
# Evaluate models
lr_accuracy, lr_report = evaluate_model(lr_model, X_test, y_test)
dt_accuracy, dt_report = evaluate_model(dt_model, X_test, y_test)
rf_accuracy, rf_report = evaluate_model(rf_model, X_test, y_test)
```

```
# Define a function to evaluate models
def evaluate_model(model, X_test, y_test):
    y_pred = model.predict(X_test)
    accuracy = accuracy_score(y_test, y_pred)
    report = classification_report(y_test, y_pred)
    return accuracy, report
```

Figure 11.16 Code snippet for model evaluation.

11.8 FURTHER LEARNING

In the future, we may investigate other ensemble learning methods in addition to simple bagging. These may include boosting (also known as AdaBoost and Gradient Boosting) and stacking, both of which have the potential to substantially improve model performance and robustness. Deepening your expertise in transforming and selecting features can help increase the interpretability and predictive power of models. Even feature engineering and selection can help with this.

```
# Evaluate models
from sklearn.metrics import accuracy_score, classification_report
lr_accuracy, lr_report = evaluate_model(lr_model, X_test, y_test)
dt_accuracy, dt_report = evaluate_model(dt_model, X_test, y_test)
rf_accuracy, rf_report = evaluate_model(rf_model, X_test, y_test)

# Print evaluation results
print("Logistic Regression Accuracy:", lr_accuracy)
print(lr_report)

print("Decision Tree Accuracy:", dt_accuracy)
print(dt_report)

print("Random Forest Accuracy:", rf_accuracy)
print(rf_report)
```

```
Logistic Regression Accuracy: 0.7921433494141971
              precision    recall  f1-score   support

           0       0.82      0.89      0.85      4839
           1       0.73      0.60      0.66      2416

    accuracy                           0.79      7255
   macro avg       0.77      0.74      0.75      7255
weighted avg       0.79      0.79      0.79      7255

Decision Tree Accuracy: 0.8690558235699517
              precision    recall  f1-score   support

           0       0.90      0.90      0.90      4839
           1       0.80      0.80      0.80      2416

    accuracy                           0.87      7255
   macro avg       0.85      0.85      0.85      7255
weighted avg       0.87      0.87      0.87      7255

Random Forest Accuracy: 0.9032391454169538
              precision    recall  f1-score   support

           0       0.91      0.95      0.93      4839
           1       0.90      0.80      0.85      2416

    accuracy                           0.90      7255
   macro avg       0.90      0.88      0.89      7255
weighted avg       0.90      0.90      0.90      7255
```

Figure 11.17 Model evaluation and comparison.

```
# Create a bar chart to compare model accuracies
model_names = ['Logistic Regression', 'Decision Tree', 'Random Forest']
accuracies = [lr_accuracy, dt_accuracy, rf_accuracy]

plt.figure(figsize=(10, 6))
plt.bar(model_names, accuracies, color='red')
plt.title('Model Comparison - Accuracy')
plt.ylim(0.5, 1.0)
plt.ylabel('Accuracy')
plt.show()
```

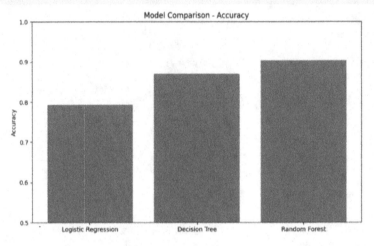

Figure 11.18 Comparing model accuracies.

SUGGESTED READING

Chatfield, C., 1986. Exploratory data analysis. *European Journal of Operational Research*, 23(1), pp.5–13.

Chapter 12

Crop recommendation prediction

LEARNING OBJECTIVES

After concluding this chapter, the reader shall be able to:

- Address the challenge on crop recommendation through an ensemble learning method.
- Build and integrate data analysis and predictive modeling.

12.1 INTRODUCTION

This chapter addresses the challenges faced on crop recommendation through an ensemble learning method. We predict the best suitable crop for a given set of soil and environmental properties. The dataset can be accessed using this link: www.kaggle.com/datasets/atharvaingle/crop-recommendation-data set. This project lays the path for the next phase of precision farming, where technology meets cultivation to alter the way crops are picked and cultivated for maximum yields and ecological harmony. This research does this by integrating data analysis, preprocessing, and predictive modeling.

12.2 DATA PREPROCESSING

Importing the necessary libraries makes it easier to manipulate data, visualize it, develop models, and assess them.

Pandas, numpy, matplotlib for visualization, and numerous classifiers from scikit-Learn are some of these packages (see Figure 12.1).

We then use the pd.read_csv as seen in Figure 12.2 to load the dataset to a variable data.

After loading our dataset we use the head() function as illustrated in Figure 12.3 from the pandas library. This function will print the first five rows from our dataset. We get a clear initial idea about our dataset after this step. We have eight columns in our dataset and label is our target column; the label column has to be encoded since it has string values.

```
# Import necessary libraries
import pandas as pd
import numpy as np
import matplotlib.pyplot as plt
from sklearn.model_selection import train_test_split
from sklearn.preprocessing import LabelEncoder
from sklearn.ensemble import BaggingClassifier
from sklearn.tree import DecisionTreeClassifier
from sklearn.ensemble import RandomForestClassifier
from sklearn.neighbors import KNeighborsClassifier
from sklearn.svm import SVC
from sklearn.linear_model import LogisticRegression
from sklearn.metrics import accuracy_score
```

Figure 12.1 Code snippet to import necessary libraries.

```
[2] # Load the crop recommendation dataset (replace 'crop_data.csv' with your file)
    data = pd.read_csv('/content/Crop_recommendation.csv')
```

Figure 12.2 Code snippet to load the dataset.

```
[3]  data.head() # print first 5 rows from the dataset
```

	N	P	K	temperature	humidity	ph	rainfall	label
0	90	42	43	20.879744	82.002744	6.502985	202.935536	rice
1	85	58	41	21.770462	80.319644	7.038096	226.655537	rice
2	60	55	44	23.004459	82.320763	7.840207	263.964248	rice
3	74	35	40	26.491096	80.158363	6.980401	242.864034	rice
4	78	42	42	20.130175	81.604873	7.628473	262.717340	rice

Figure 12.3 Using head() function.

To find out the number of missing or null values in each column of our dataset we use the isnull().sum() function to count the null values. In our dataset we don't have any missing values (see Figure 12.4).

Previously we found there is a need to encode the label column. We use the LabelEncoder (https://scikit-learn.org/stable/modules/generated/sklearn. preprocessing.LabelEncoder.html) as in Figure 12.5 from scikit-learn for

```
data.isnull().sum() # calculating the null values in each columns

N                0
P                0
K                0
temperature      0
humidity         0
ph               0
rainfall         0
label            0
dtype: int64
```

Figure 12.4 To find missing values in the dataset.

```
le = LabelEncoder()
data['label_encoded'] = le.fit_transform(data['label'])
X = data.drop(['label'], axis=1)
y = data['label']
```

Figure 12.5 Encoding the label column.

this task. The method uses unique numerical values to convert the categorical columns to numeric. The resulting dataset is stored in a variable named "label_encoded." We then create two variables, X and y. In X we store all the features and drop the target variable and in y we store only the target variable.

12.3 DATA SPLITTING

As we have already separated our dataset to X and y in the previous step, now we split the dataset into training and testing sets using the train_test_ split function from scikit-learn. As discussed, X and y contain feature matrix and target vector respectively. The test size is 20% and train size is 80% as denoted in Figure 12.6. The random state sets the seed for reproducibility.

12.4 INITIALIZE BASE CLASSIFIERS AND BAGGING MODELS

For modeling we have used the bootstrap aggregating method also known as bagging, which is an ensemble learning technique to boost accuracy and performance of our models. This is achieved by combining the predictions of multiple base models to make the overall prediction more accurate.

```
[6] # Split the data into training and testing sets
    X_train, X_test, y_train, y_test = train_test_split(X, y, test_size=0.2, random_state=42)
```

Figure 12.6 Code snippet to split the dataset.

```
# Initialize base classifiers
base_classifiers = [
    KNeighborsClassifier(),
    SVC(),
    LogisticRegression()
]

# Initialize Bagging models with base classifiers
bagging_models = [
    BaggingClassifier(base_classifier, n_estimators=10, random_state=42)
    for base_classifier in base_classifiers
]
```

Figure 12.7 Code snippet to initialize base classifiers.

The base classifiers used are KNN, SVC and Logistic regression models which will act as weak learner for the bagging ensemble. The n_estimators specify the number of base classifiers. This will allow the models to learn finding the optimized solution and diverse errors enhancing overall performance. Refer to Figure 12.7 for the code snippet.

12.5 TRAINING

We initiate a loop which trains and evaluates a series of bagging models that has been initialized by us. We use the fit method to train data and predict target using the predict method. The accuracy of all the models is computed and stored in a list called accuracies as depicted in Figure 12.8.

12.6 EVALUATION AND COMPARISON

A list called model_names is created as shown in Figure 12.9 and the three model names are stored in it.

Finally, we generate a bar plot as specified in Figure 12.10 to compare the accuracies of different models visually. Each bar present in the graph depicts different models and their accuracies. Logistic regression is the best performing model with respect to this dataset.

```
# Train and evaluate bagging models
accuracies = []
for model in bagging_models:
    model.fit(X_train, y_train)
    y_pred = model.predict(X_test)
    accuracy = accuracy_score(y_test, y_pred)
    accuracies.append(accuracy)

/usr/local/lib/python3.10/dist-packages/sklearn/linear_model/_logistic.py:458: ConvergenceWarning: lbfgs failed to converge (status=1):
STOP: TOTAL NO. of ITERATIONS REACHED LIMIT.

Increase the number of iterations (max_iter) or scale the data as shown in:
```

Figure 12.8 Model training and evaluation.

```
# Model names for plotting
model_names = [ 'K-Nearest Neighbors', 'Support Vector Machine', 'Logistic Regression']
```

Figure 12.9 Model names for plotting.

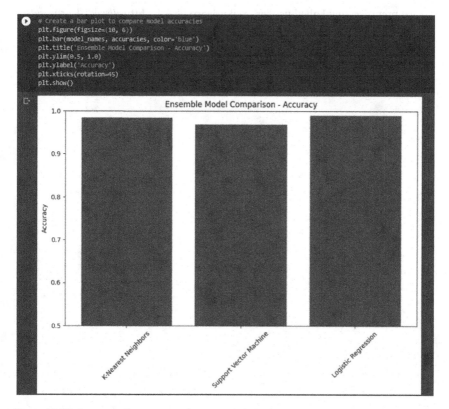

```
# Create a bar plot to compare model accuracies
plt.figure(figsize=(10, 6))
plt.bar(model_names, accuracies, color='blue')
plt.title('Ensemble Model Comparison - Accuracy')
plt.ylim(0.5, 1.0)
plt.ylabel('Accuracy')
plt.xticks(rotation=45)
plt.show()
```

Figure 12.10 Accuracy Comparison.

12.7 CONCLUSION

This chapter delivers a thorough understanding of ensemble learning, bagging, and model evaluation, laying the groundwork for well-informed decision-making across a variety of domains. By enabling more precise and effective agricultural operations, the use of ensemble approaches to crop recommendation serves as an example of how machine learning can change agriculture.

12.8 FURTHER LEARNING

Consider exploring more complex ensemble techniques like Random Forests and Gradient Boosting, which provide improved predictive power through combined decision trees, for further development in the field of crop recommendation. Explore feature engineering to glean insightful information from agricultural data, and hyperparameter optimization to enhance model efficiency.

SUGGESTED READING

sklearn.preprocessing.LabelEncoder, scikit-learn 1.4.1, https://scikit-learn.org/stable/modules/generated/sklearn.preprocessing.LabelEncoder.html

Chapter 13

Brain tumor classification

LEARNING OBJECTIVES

After concluding this chapter, the reader shall be able to:

- Solve image classification problem with the aid of deep learning models.
- Train, test and classify the machine learning models.

13.1 INTRODUCTION

The main goal of this chapter is to demonstrate to the readers how to solve an image classification problem through the development of deep learning models. Medical image classification is a key part of the healthcare field. Diseases can be better diagnosed and treated if they are identified and put into categories. This will save lives, especially when brain cancers are found early. This project uses a set of MRI pictures of brain tumors as its dataset. It has pictures of different kinds of tumors and pictures that don't have tumors. This collection gives us a great way to train and test our machine learning models. The dataset from Kaggle at www.kaggle.com/datasets/sartajbhuvaji/brain-tumor-classification-mri is used for this task. For this classification job, we use VGG16 and ResNet50, which are both well-known architectures. The models will be taught to put MRI pictures into four different groups: "glioma_tumor," "meningioma_tumor," "no_tumor," and "pituitary_tumor."

13.2 DATA PREPROCESSING

We start by importing the necessary libraries for our classification task. The module will give us a way to interact with file paths, dictionaries, etc. numpy is imported to handle numerical operations, and matplotlib is used for visualizations and plots. Then we import the tensorflow module, which allows us to train the neural network frameworks. Followed by two of the

```
import os
import numpy as np
import matplotlib.pyplot as plt
import tensorflow as tf
from tensorflow.keras.preprocessing.image import ImageDataGenerator
from tensorflow.keras.applications import VGG16, ResNet50
from tensorflow.keras.models import Sequential
from tensorflow.keras.layers import GlobalAveragePooling2D, Dense, Dropout
```

Figure 13.1 To import necessary libraries.

```
pip install opendatasets

Collecting opendatasets
  Downloading opendatasets-0.1.22-py3-none-any.whl (15 kB)
Requirement already satisfied: tqdm in /usr/local/lib/python3.10/dist-packages (from opendatasets) (4.66.1)
```

Figure 13.2 Code snippet to collect open datasets.

```
import opendatasets as od

od.download("https://www.kaggle.com/datasets/sartajbhuvaji/brain-tumor-classification-mri")

Please provide your Kaggle credentials to download this dataset. Learn more: http://bit.ly/kaggle-creds
Your Kaggle username: akshaybr
Your Kaggle Key: ··········
Downloading brain-tumor-classification-mri.zip to ./brain-tumor-classification-mri
100%|██████████| 86.8M/86.8M [00:03<00:00, 29.6MB/s]
```

Figure 13.3 To import opendatasets libraries.

pretrained models, VGG16 and ResNet50 from keras. Sequential is an API for building DNN models layer by layer. GlobalAveragePooling2D and Dense are the layers, and Dropout is to prevent overfitting. All can be seen in Figure 13.1.

We then install the command opendatasets for downloading datasets that are openly available. We can fetch datasets online after this (see Figure 13.2).

Then we import the opendatasets library as od. We use the dataset link from Kaggle to download the Brain Tumor Classification Dataset. Before this step, make sure you download the Kaggle API credentials in your Kaggle account settings. The necessary steps are provided in Figure 13.3.

Two different variables, data_dir and classes, are declared, where the "data_dir" variable contains the path to training data and "classes" contains the list of class labels for the image classification task. The code snippet for this is depicted in Figure 13.4.

```
# Define the paths to your data
data_dir = '/content/brain-tumor-classification-mri/Training'
classes = ['glioma_tumor', 'meningioma_tumor', 'no_tumor', 'pituitary_tumor']
```

Figure 13.4 Code snippet to define paths.

We generate a visual display from our test images of brain tumor classes randomly as shown in Figure 13.5.

In this step, we set two of the hyperparameters, batch size and epochs, for training our models. The same can be seen in Figure 13.6. The batch size defines the number of samples that will be used during the forward and backward passes in the training phase. The epochs define the number of times the training takes place to update the model's weights. We have to note that training the model with a large number of epochs will lead to over training. Likewise, training a few will lead to underfitting.

We use the ImageDataGenerator class to clean and add to the data, and we make two data producers for the training and validation sets. ImageDataGenerator changes images in different ways, like resizing, rotating, etc., to add more variety to our collection. "flow_from_directory" is used to make the "train_generator" for the training set. It looks for all the training pictures in the data_dir directory. The size of the target picture is set to (224, 224), which is the same as the size of the input for models like VGG16 and ResNet50. The class_mode is set to "categorical" because we have more than one class. Based on the validation_split parameter, the training part of the data is chosen by setting the group parameter to "training." We made a validation data generator with the same settings as train_generator. Refer to Figure 13.7 for the code snippet.

13.3 MODELING

We move on to create a VGG16-based neural network model as seen in Figure 13.8. We initialize by setting weights, excluding the output layer and specifying the input shape matching our input images and we stack all the layers sequentially. Finally, we compile the model.

Following the same previous steps, the ResNet50 (Mukti and Biswas, 2019) model is also initialized with the process as provided in Figure 13.9.

By calling the fit method we started training our VGG16 model (Qassim et al., 2018). This code as given in Figure 13.10 will train the model using training data generator and validate the model using validation data generator for 20 epochs.

```
import os
import random
import matplotlib.pyplot as plt
from PIL import Image
main_folder = '/content/brain-tumor-classification-mri/Testing'
class_labels = ['glioma_tumor', 'meningioma_tumor', 'no_tumor', 'pituitary_tumor']
rows, cols = 2, 3
fig, axes = plt.subplots(rows, cols, figsize=(10, 6))
for ax in axes.ravel():
    class_label = random.choice(class_labels)
    class_folder = os.path.join(main_folder, class_label)
    image_files = os.listdir(class_folder)
    random_image = random.choice(image_files)
    image_path = os.path.join(class_folder, random_image)
    image = Image.open(image_path)
    ax.imshow(image)
    ax.set_title(class_label)
    ax.axis('off')
plt.subplots_adjust(wspace=0.2, hspace=0.3)
plt.show()
```

Figure 13.5 Visual display of test images.

```
# Set hyperparameters
batch_size = 32
epochs = 20
```

Figure 13.6 Setting hyperparameters.

```
# Data preprocessing and augmentation
datagen = ImageDataGenerator(
    rescale=1.0/255.0,
    rotation_range=20,
    width_shift_range=0.2,
    height_shift_range=0.2,
    horizontal_flip=True,
    validation_split=0.2
)

train_generator = datagen.flow_from_directory(
    data_dir,
    target_size=(224, 224),  # VGG16 and ResNet50 input size
    batch_size=batch_size,
    class_mode='categorical',
    subset='training'
)

validation_generator = datagen.flow_from_directory(
    data_dir,
    target_size=(224, 224),
    batch_size=batch_size,
    class_mode='categorical',
    subset='validation'
)
```

```
Found 2297 images belonging to 4 classes.
Found 573 images belonging to 4 classes.
```

Figure 13.7 Data preprocessing and augmentation.

```
# Create and compile VGG16 model
base_model_vgg16 = VGG16(weights='imagenet', include_top=False, input_shape=(224, 224, 3))
model_vgg16 = Sequential([
    base_model_vgg16,
    GlobalAveragePooling2D(),
    Dense(512, activation='relu'),
    Dropout(0.5),
    Dense(len(classes), activation='softmax')
])
model_vgg16.compile(optimizer='adam', loss='categorical_crossentropy', metrics=['accuracy'])
```

Figure 13.8 To create a VGG16 model.

```
# Create and compile ResNet50 model
base_model_resnet50 = ResNet50(weights='imagenet', include_top=False, input_shape=(224, 224, 3))
model_resnet50 = Sequential([
    base_model_resnet50,
    GlobalAveragePooling2D(),
    Dense(512, activation='relu'),
    Dropout(0.5),
    Dense(len(classes), activation='softmax')
])
model_resnet50.compile(optimizer='adam', loss='categorical_crossentropy', metrics=['accuracy'])
```

Figure 13.9 To create a ResNet50 model.

```
# Train the models
history_vgg16 = model_vgg16.fit(train_generator, epochs=epochs, validation_data=validation_generator)

Epoch 1/20
72/72 [==============================] - 53s 659ms/step - loss: 1.4903 - accuracy: 0.2978 - val_loss: 1.3426 - val_accuracy: 0.3717
Epoch 2/20
72/72 [==============================] - 47s 654ms/step - loss: 1.2980 - accuracy: 0.3670 - val_loss: 1.3093 - val_accuracy: 0.3089
Epoch 3/20
72/72 [==============================] - 50s 695ms/step - loss: 1.2520 - accuracy: 0.4014 - val_loss: 1.2568 - val_accuracy: 0.4084
Epoch 4/20
72/72 [==============================] - 46s 634ms/step - loss: 1.2422 - accuracy: 0.4079 - val_loss: 1.2399 - val_accuracy: 0.4241
Epoch 5/20
72/72 [==============================] - 47s 646ms/step - loss: 1.1591 - accuracy: 0.4528 - val_loss: 1.2162 - val_accuracy: 0.4695
Epoch 6/20
72/72 [==============================] - 48s 661ms/step - loss: 1.1288 - accuracy: 0.4819 - val_loss: 1.2811 - val_accuracy: 0.3997
Epoch 7/20
72/72 [==============================] - 46s 632ms/step - loss: 1.1040 - accuracy: 0.5024 - val_loss: 1.2712 - val_accuracy: 0.5026
Epoch 8/20
72/72 [==============================] - 47s 647ms/step - loss: 1.0339 - accuracy: 0.5403 - val_loss: 1.1495 - val_accuracy: 0.5288
Epoch 9/20
72/72 [==============================] - 48s 661ms/step - loss: 1.0010 - accuracy: 0.5694 - val_loss: 1.1055 - val_accuracy: 0.5166
Epoch 10/20
72/72 [==============================] - 46s 645ms/step - loss: 0.9467 - accuracy: 0.6091 - val_loss: 1.1823 - val_accuracy: 0.4939
Epoch 11/20
72/72 [==============================] - 46s 632ms/step - loss: 1.0754 - accuracy: 0.5263 - val_loss: 1.1127 - val_accuracy: 0.5148
Epoch 12/20
72/72 [==============================] - 46s 633ms/step - loss: 0.9720 - accuracy: 0.5760 - val_loss: 1.0208 - val_accuracy: 0.6021
Epoch 13/20
72/72 [==============================] - 48s 663ms/step - loss: 0.8742 - accuracy: 0.6552 - val_loss: 0.9895 - val_accuracy: 0.6335
Epoch 14/20
72/72 [==============================] - 47s 650ms/step - loss: 0.8733 - accuracy: 0.6421 - val_loss: 1.0112 - val_accuracy: 0.5916
Epoch 15/20
72/72 [==============================] - 46s 636ms/step - loss: 0.8125 - accuracy: 0.6717 - val_loss: 0.9620 - val_accuracy: 0.6387
Epoch 16/20
72/72 [==============================] - 48s 656ms/step - loss: 0.7897 - accuracy: 0.6983 - val_loss: 1.0348 - val_accuracy: 0.6126
Epoch 17/20
72/72 [==============================] - 47s 645ms/step - loss: 0.7979 - accuracy: 0.6870 - val_loss: 1.1835 - val_accuracy: 0.5305
Epoch 18/20
72/72 [==============================] - 47s 647ms/step - loss: 0.7339 - accuracy: 0.7240 - val_loss: 0.9301 - val_accuracy: 0.6370
Epoch 19/20
72/72 [==============================] - 47s 646ms/step - loss: 0.6722 - accuracy: 0.7366 - val_loss: 1.0859 - val_accuracy: 0.5899
Epoch 20/20
72/72 [==============================] - 47s 649ms/step - loss: 0.6748 - accuracy: 0.7366 - val_loss: 0.8444 - val_accuracy: 0.6928
```

Figure 13.10 Training the VGG16 model.

Using the same method followed earlier, we train the ResNet-50 model too as seen in Figure 13.11.

13.4 TRAINING ACCURACY COMPARISON

A line plot is generated using the above code as in Figure 13.12. The training epochs are represented in the X-axis and Y-axis represents the accuracy.

```
history_resnet50 = model_resnet50.fit(train_generator, epochs=epochs, validation_data=validation_generator)

Epoch 1/20
72/72 [==============================] - 83s 649ms/step - loss: 0.9632 - accuracy: 0.6613 - val_loss: 38.1912 - val_accuracy: 0.2880
Epoch 2/20
72/72 [==============================] - 49s 680ms/step - loss: 0.5385 - accuracy: 0.7980 - val_loss: 4.4422 - val_accuracy: 0.2862
Epoch 3/20
72/72 [==============================] - 44s 612ms/step - loss: 0.4142 - accuracy: 0.8463 - val_loss: 4.4865 - val_accuracy: 0.1379
Epoch 4/20
72/72 [==============================] - 45s 629ms/step - loss: 0.3277 - accuracy: 0.8872 - val_loss: 4.9291 - val_accuracy: 0.1379
Epoch 5/20
72/72 [==============================] - 47s 659ms/step - loss: 0.2744 - accuracy: 0.9121 - val_loss: 8.3081 - val_accuracy: 0.1379
Epoch 6/20
72/72 [==============================] - 45s 627ms/step - loss: 0.2740 - accuracy: 0.9081 - val_loss: 2.9952 - val_accuracy: 0.1379
Epoch 7/20
72/72 [==============================] - 44s 609ms/step - loss: 0.2570 - accuracy: 0.9055 - val_loss: 8.9786 - val_accuracy: 0.1379
Epoch 8/20
72/72 [==============================] - 45s 630ms/step - loss: 0.1982 - accuracy: 0.9303 - val_loss: 7.0889 - val_accuracy: 0.1291
Epoch 9/20
72/72 [==============================] - 45s 618ms/step - loss: 0.2223 - accuracy: 0.9164 - val_loss: 7.7013 - val_accuracy: 0.1326
Epoch 10/20
72/72 [==============================] - 45s 619ms/step - loss: 0.1954 - accuracy: 0.9325 - val_loss: 7.3896 - val_accuracy: 0.4747
Epoch 11/20
72/72 [==============================] - 46s 631ms/step - loss: 0.1763 - accuracy: 0.9404 - val_loss: 11.7994 - val_accuracy: 0.1379
Epoch 12/20
72/72 [==============================] - 45s 628ms/step - loss: 0.1680 - accuracy: 0.9443 - val_loss: 39.9150 - val_accuracy: 0.3072
Epoch 13/20
72/72 [==============================] - 45s 619ms/step - loss: 0.1633 - accuracy: 0.9486 - val_loss: 4.8782 - val_accuracy: 0.3892
Epoch 14/20
72/72 [==============================] - 45s 625ms/step - loss: 0.1518 - accuracy: 0.9451 - val_loss: 3.3225 - val_accuracy: 0.4782
Epoch 15/20
72/72 [==============================] - 44s 615ms/step - loss: 0.1547 - accuracy: 0.9508 - val_loss: 2.6496 - val_accuracy: 0.5393
Epoch 16/20
72/72 [==============================] - 46s 638ms/step - loss: 0.1579 - accuracy: 0.9478 - val_loss: 3.0259 - val_accuracy: 0.3194
Epoch 17/20
72/72 [==============================] - 45s 625ms/step - loss: 0.1435 - accuracy: 0.9595 - val_loss: 0.7652 - val_accuracy: 0.7906
Epoch 18/20
72/72 [==============================] - 48s 661ms/step - loss: 0.1473 - accuracy: 0.9573 - val_loss: 13.4199 - val_accuracy: 0.2304
Epoch 19/20
72/72 [==============================] - 46s 631ms/step - loss: 0.1351 - accuracy: 0.9604 - val_loss: 1.0012 - val_accuracy: 0.7155
Epoch 20/20
72/72 [==============================] - 44s 614ms/step - loss: 0.1365 - accuracy: 0.9517 - val_loss: 1.0100 - val_accuracy: 0.7260
```

Figure 13.11 Training the ResNet-50 model.

The VGG16-based model is trained and evaluated, yielding the following results:

- Training accuracy: 73.66%
- Validation accuracy: 69.28%

The ResNet50-based model is also trained and evaluated, resulting in the following outcomes:

- Training accuracy: 95.17%
- Validation accuracy: 72.60%

13.5 CONCLUSION

The findings of this chapter highlight the utility of deep learning models, in particular VGG16 and ResNet50, for the categorization of brain cancers based on MRI scans. Both models obtain encouraging levels of training accuracy, indicating that they are able to acquire relevant features by studying medical images.

```
# Plot training accuracy
plt.plot(history_vgg16.history['accuracy'], label='VGG16 Training Accuracy')
plt.plot(history_resnet50.history['accuracy'], label='ResNet50 Training Accuracy')
plt.xlabel('Epoch')
plt.ylabel('Accuracy')
plt.legend()
plt.show()
```

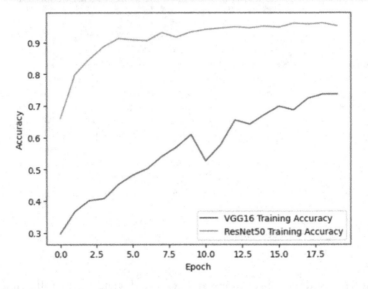

Figure 13.12 Training accuracy plot.

13.6 FURTHER WORKS

Possible topics for further research in this field include:

- Evaluation of the performance of the model using a separate test dataset in great detail.
- Adjusting the model's hyperparameters to get optimal generalization performance.
- Methods of interpretability that allow for the gaining of insights into model decisions.
- Implementation of a trained model as an integral component of a medical diagnosis system, accompanied by exhaustive clinical validation.

The application of machine learning to medical diagnosis carries with it a vast amount of untapped potential, making continued study in this field absolutely necessary for the advancement of patient care.

SUGGESTED READINGS

Mukti, I.Z. and Biswas, D., 2019, December. Transfer learning based plant diseases detection using ResNet50. In *2019 4th International Conference on Electrical Information and Communication Technology (EICT)* (pp.1–6). IEEE.

Qassim, H., Verma, A. and Feinzimer, D., 2018, January. Compressed residual-VGG16 CNN model for big data places image recognition. In *2018 IEEE 8th Annual Computing and Communication Workshop and Conference (CCWC)* (pp.169–175). IEEE.

Chapter 14

Exploratory data analysis and classification on wine quality dataset with oneAPI

LEARNING OBJECTIVES

After reading this chapter, the reader shall be able to:

- Acquire the knowledge to examine wine quality and classification through machine learning techniques by developing predictive models.
- Gain information regarding exploratory data analysis.

14.1 INTRODUCTION

This study entails a thorough examination of wine quality and classification through the utilization of machine learning techniques. Our methodology is built on the bedrock of exploratory data analysis, also known as EDA. We perform an exhaustive investigation of the dataset's complexities using EDA, which enables us to unearth previously concealed patterns, possible outliers, and important correlations between variables. The main objective of our study is to develop predictive models that can accurately forecast the quality of wine using a dataset comprising diverse parameters. In order to do this task, the initial step involves importing crucial libraries that are necessary for data manipulation, visualisation, and machine learning. These libraries include pandas, numpy, matplotlib, seaborn, and scikit-learn. The dataset, "WineQT.csv," which is taken from kaggle: https://www.kag gle.com/datasets/yasserh/wine-quality-dataset is loaded and subjected to preliminary data exploration in order to acquire a comprehensive understanding of its underlying structure.

14.2 EXPLORATORY DATA ANALYSIS (EDA)

We engage in exploratory data analysis, also known as EDA, in order to acquire a more in-depth comprehension of our dataset. During this step, we create visualizations of the data such as histograms, box plots, and pair

DOI: 10.1201/9781032676685-15

```
[ ]   # Import necessary libraries
      import pandas as pd
      import numpy as np
      import matplotlib.pyplot as plt
      import seaborn as sns
      from sklearn.model_selection import train_test_split
      from sklearn.ensemble import RandomForestClassifier, GradientBoostingClassifier
      from sklearn.tree import DecisionTreeClassifier
      from sklearn.metrics import accuracy_score
      from imblearn.over_sampling import SMOTE
      from sklearn.utils.class_weight import compute_class_weight
```

Figure 14.1 Importing the necessary libraries.

plots in order to discover patterns, relationships, and potential outliers in the information. These visualizations provide useful insights into the characteristics of wine, including the distribution of certain characteristics, the influence of characteristics on wine quality, and more.

The provided code as seen in Figure 14.1 primarily imports various Python libraries necessary for conducting data analysis and machine learning tasks, which are essential for this chapter. The seaborn and matplotlib libraries are commonly employed for the purpose of data visualization, while sklearn is utilized for machine learning operations. Additionally, pandas and numpy are employed for data manipulation and processing.

Next, the dataset WineQT.csv is imported from Kaggle using the pd.read_ csv function, and afterwards stored in a pandas data frame. Then we use the .head() function to look at the first five rows of the dataset for initial analysis. Refer to Figure 14.2.

In order to conduct a comprehensive examination of the numerical columns inside our dataset, we utilize the "describe()" function to obtain statistical measures such as the mean, standard deviation, minimum, maximum, and count and the same is shown in Figure 14.3.

The alcohol concentration in wine is a significant determinant of its overall quality. In order to achieve a high level of quality, it is imperative that the subject matter be presented in a well-balanced manner. Now, let us proceed with the analysis of the alcohol characteristics. Initially, the sns. histplot function is employed to generate a histogram, which serves the purpose of visually representing the distribution of the alcohol characteristic as illustrated in Figure 14.4.

Next, a boxplot is generated in order to assess the dispersion, skewness, and presence of outliers within our dataset. The sns.boxplot function is utilized to generate boxplots representing the distribution of alcohol and density across various degrees of wine quality. The visual representation depicted in the Figure 14.5 showcases black dots that are indicative of outliers.

```
[2]: data= pd.read_csv("WineQT.csv")
```

```
[3]: data.head()
```

[3]:

	fixed acidity	volatile acidity	citric acid	residual sugar	chlorides	free sulfur dioxide	total sulfur dioxide	density	pH	sulphates	alcohol	quality	Id
0	7.4	0.70	0.00	1.9	0.076	11.0	34.0	0.9978	3.51	0.56	9.4	5	0
1	7.8	0.88	0.00	2.6	0.098	25.0	67.0	0.9968	3.20	0.68	9.8	5	1
2	7.8	0.76	0.04	2.3	0.092	15.0	54.0	0.9970	3.26	0.65	9.8	5	2
3	11.2	0.28	0.56	1.9	0.075	17.0	60.0	0.9980	3.16	0.58	9.8	6	3
4	7.4	0.70	0.00	1.9	0.076	11.0	34.0	0.9978	3.51	0.56	9.4	5	4

Figure 14.2 Code snippet to load the dataset.

```
[4]: data.describe()
```

[4]:

	fixed acidity	volatile acidity	citric acid	residual sugar	chlorides	free sulfur dioxide	total sulfur dioxide	density	pH	sulphates	alcohol
count	1143.000000	1143.000000	1143.000000	1143.000000	1143.000000	1143.000000	1143.000000	1143.000000	1143.000000	1143.000000	1143.000000
mean	8.311111	0.531339	0.268364	2.532152	0.086933	15.615486	45.914698	0.996730	3.311015	0.657708	10.442111
std	1.747595	0.179633	0.196686	1.355917	0.047267	10.250486	32.782130	0.001925	0.156664	0.170399	1.082196
min	4.600000	0.120000	0.000000	0.900000	0.012000	1.000000	6.000000	0.990070	2.740000	0.330000	8.400000
25%	7.100000	0.392500	0.090000	1.900000	0.070000	7.000000	21.000000	0.995570	3.205000	0.550000	9.500000
50%	7.900000	0.520000	0.250000	2.200000	0.079000	13.000000	37.000000	0.996680	3.310000	0.620000	10.200000
75%	9.100000	0.640000	0.420000	2.600000	0.090000	21.000000	61.000000	0.997845	3.400000	0.730000	11.100000
max	15.900000	1.580000	1.000000	15.500000	0.611000	68.000000	289.000000	1.003690	4.010000	2.000000	14.900000

Figure 14.3 Using describe() function.

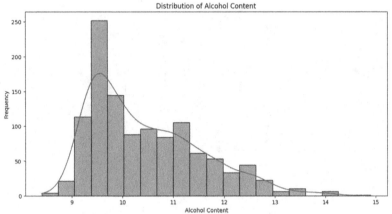

Figure 14.4 Generating a histogram.

In order to examine the associations between various features, it is possible to build a pairplot as represented in Figure 14.6. In this analysis, the sns.pairplot function is employed to examine the association between the variables "fixed acidity" and "volatile acidity," with a specific emphasis on their relationship with the variable "quality."

In this part, a pie chart displaying the distribution of wine quality levels throughout the dataset is created as in Figure 14.7 with the help of the plt. pie function.

A table that summarizes the correlation coefficients between a number of different variables is known as a correlation matrix. In the fields of statistics and data analysis, it is a typical method that is used to investigate the correlations that exist between numerous variables at the same time. With the help of the data.corr() function, a correlation matrix of the dataset is created as in Figure 14.8. Then, it builds a heatmap for visualizing the correlation between the various features by making use of the sns.heatmap package.

14.3 DATA PREPROCESSING AND SPLITTING

We use the isnull().sum() command as illustrated in Figure 14.9 to look at the null values present in the dataset. Here there are no null values present.

The next step in processing our dataset is to separate it into a training set and a testing set. The train_test_split function found in the sklearn library

```
[6]: # Box plots for wine quality vs. features
     quality_vs_features = ['alcohol', 'density']
     for feature in quality_vs_features:
         plt.figure(figsize=(5, 2))
         sns.boxplot(x='quality', y=feature, data=data)
         plt.title(f'{feature} vs. Quality')
         plt.xlabel('Quality')
         plt.ylabel(feature)
         plt.show()
```

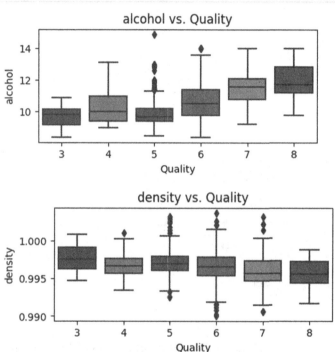

Figure 14.5 Generating a boxplot.

is what we turn to in order to accomplish this. First, all of the features are entered into variable X, and the target column is entered into variable y. The feature data and the target data for both sets are stored in the variables X_train, X_test, y_train, and y_test respectively. Using the compute_class_weight function from sklearn will do the calculation to determine class weights in order to address class imbalance. It makes use of the "balanced" technique and computes weights for each of the classes contained in the training data. Refer to Figure 14.10 for the same.

```
[7]: # Pairplot to visualize relationships between features
     sns.pairplot(data, vars=['fixed acidity', 'volatile acidity'], hue='quality')
     plt.suptitle('Pairplot of Features by Wine Quality', y=1.02)
     plt.show()
```

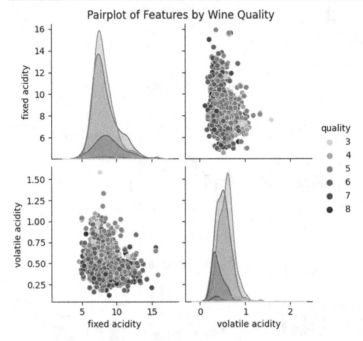

Figure 14.6 Building a pairplot.

14.4 MODELING

After that, we use a technique called the Synthetic Minority Over-sampling Technique (SMOTE) to oversample the minority classes in the training data as shown in Figure 14.11. This allows us to get results that are more accurate. The SMOTE class found in the imblearn library is utilized by it. Then, we generate a list and initialize each model by employing the Random Forest, Decision Tree, and Gradient Boosting classifiers respectively. These models are going to undergo training and testing. Additionally, in order to get superior overall performance, each of these models has been tuned with oneAPI. In this case, we optimize using the one Data analytics library, which is abbreviated as oneDAL. The optimzation is explained in the notice that appears in a pop-up window below the cell highlighted in red.

In order to show the results, we first generate an empty dictionary and then assign it to a variable that goes by the name results as depicted in Figure 14.12. The accuracy scores of our trained models will be stored here.

```
[8]: # Pie chart for wine type distribution
     wine_type_counts = data['quality'].value_counts()
     plt.figure(figsize=(6, 6))
     plt.pie(wine_type_counts, labels=wine_type_counts.index, autopct='%1.1f%%', startangle=140)
     plt.title('Distribution of Wine Types')
     plt.show()
```

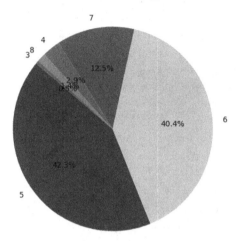

Figure 14.7 pie chart display.

After going through all of the models, the loop inserts the relevant results into the results dictionary as it proceeds to iterate through the models.

14.5 MODEL COMPARISON AND VISUALIZATION

The accuracy score for each model that is stored in the results dictionary is printed by this loop. Figure 14.13 illustrates the same.

In this section, we will assess the accuracy of several different models by generating a bar plot as seen in Figure 14.14 with the sns.barplot package. For the purpose of making this comparison, it consults the accuracy scores that are saved in the results dictionary.

14.6 CONCLUSION

Here we have provided a synopsis of the most important findings and outcomes of the chapter. We have explained any constraints or difficulties that were encountered throughout the course of the chapter and remark on the accuracy with which the machine learning models were able to forecast the wine quality. In addition to this, we investigated the models' viability for use in the actual world.

```
[9]:  # Create a correlation matrix heatmap
      correlation_matrix = data.corr()
      plt.figure(figsize=(8, 6))
      sns.heatmap(correlation_matrix, annot=True, cmap='coolwarm')
      plt.title('Correlation Matrix')
      plt.show()
```

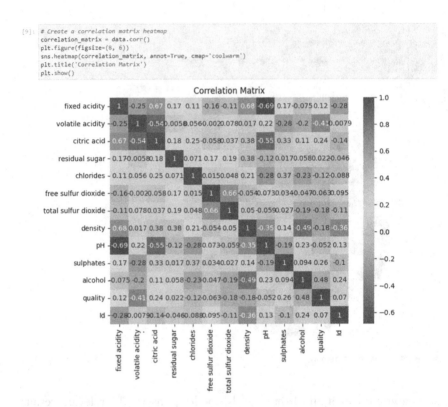

Figure 14.8 Correlation Matrix Heatmap creation.

14.7 FURTHER LEARNING

We encourage additional learning by recommending areas where the project could be extended or improved. Hopefully, this will inspire you to continue your own learning. We provide extra resources or courses for readers interested in delving deeper into machine learning and data analysis. Additionally, we provide recommendations for additional studies or methodologies that could improve the accuracy or insights provided by the models.

```
[10]: data.isnull().sum()
```

```
[10]: fixed acidity          0
      volatile acidity       0
      citric acid            0
      residual sugar         0
      chlorides              0
      free sulfur dioxide    0
      total sulfur dioxide   0
      density                0
      pH                     0
      sulphates              0
      alcohol                0
      quality                0
      Id                     0
      dtype: int64
```

Figure 14.9 Look for null values in the dataset.

```
[11]: X = data.drop(['Id'],axis=1)
      y = data['Id']
```

```
[12]:
      # Split the data into training and testing sets
      X_train, X_test, y_train, y_test = train_test_split(X, y, test_size=0.2, random_state=42)

      # Calculate class weights to address class imbalance
      class_weights = compute_class_weight('balanced', classes=np.unique(y_train), y=y_train)
```

Figure 14.10 Feature separation and dataset splitting.

```
[13]:  # Oversample the minority classes using SMOTE
       smote = SMOTE(sampling_strategy='auto', random_state=42)
       X_train_resampled, y_train_resampled = smote.fit_resample(X_train, y_train)
       from sklearnex import patch_sklearn
       patch_sklearn()
       # Create a list of classifiers
       models = [
           ("Random Forest", RandomForestClassifier(class_weight=dict(zip(np.unique(y_train_resampled), class_weights)))),
           ("Decision Tree", DecisionTreeClassifier(class_weight=dict(zip(np.unique(y_train_resampled), class_weights)), random_state=42)),
           ("Gradient Boosting", GradientBoostingClassifier(random_state=42)),
       ]
```

```
Intel(R) Extension for Scikit-learn* enabled (https://github.com/intel/scikit-learn-intelex)
```

Figure 14.11 To oversample the minority classes in the training data.

```python
# Initialize results dictionary
results = {}

# Train and evaluate each model
for model_name, model in models:
    model.fit(X_train_resampled, y_train_resampled)
    y_pred = model.predict(X_test)
    accuracy = accuracy_score(y_test, y_pred)
    results[model_name] = accuracy
```

Figure 14.12 To show the results.

```python
# Train and evaluate each model
for model_name, model in models:
    model.fit(X_train_resampled, y_train_resampled)
    y_pred = model.predict(X_test)
    accuracy = accuracy_score(y_test, y_pred)
    results[model_name] = accuracy

    # Print the accuracy score for each model
    print(f"{model_name} Accuracy: {accuracy:.2f}")
```

```
Random Forest Accuracy: 0.59
Decision Tree Accuracy: 0.59
Gradient Boosting Accuracy: 0.60
```

Figure 14.13 Training and evaluation.

```
# Create a bar plot to compare model accuracies
plt.figure(figsize=(5, 2))
sns.barplot(x=list(results.keys()), y=list(results.values()))
plt.title('Model Accuracy Comparison')
plt.xlabel('Model')
plt.ylabel('Accuracy')
plt.ylim(0.5, 1.0)  # Set y-axis limits
plt.xticks(rotation=45)
plt.show()
```

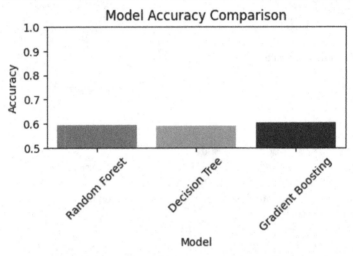

Figure 14.14 Model accuracy comparison.

## Chapter 15

Cats vs. Dogs classification using deep learning models optimized with oneAPI

LEARNING OBJECTIVES

After concluding this chapter, the reader shall be able to:

- Explore image categorization with data sets for deep learning research.
- Train and evaluate neural network architectures.

15.1 INTRODUCTION

In this chapter, we explore the wonderful world of image categorization with the Kaggle dataset Cats vs. Dogs. The dataset is available to be accessed by clicking on the following link: www.kaggle.com/datasets/ shaunthesheep/microsoft-catsvsdogs-dataset. A dataset comparing cats and dogs is chosen because it contains thousands of tagged images of cats and dogs, which is ideally suited to serve as a testing ground for deep learning research. Our objective is to train and evaluate two powerful neural network architectures, namely a proprietary Sequential model and a VGG16-based model, to determine the superior one in differentiating between the feline and canine companions that we know and love.

15.2 DATA PREPROCESSING

We begin by importing all of the libraries required for our image categorization operation. To do tasks involving data manipulation, fundamental libraries such as pandas and numpy are imported. We bring in matplotlib and seaborn so that we can do visualization. Importing the ImageDataGenerator class from TensorFlow's Keras API allows for the first processing of picture data. Additionally, to create models layer by layer we import sequential. Optimizer adam is imported. The entire code snippet is presented in Figure 15.1.

The TensorFlow library is utilized for the purpose of importing neural network models, defining layers, and conducting statistical and mathematical

DOI: 10.1201/9781032676685-16

```
import pandas as pd
import numpy as np
import matplotlib.pyplot as plt
import seaborn as sns
from tensorflow.keras.applications import VGG16
from tensorflow.keras.models import Sequential
from tensorflow.keras.layers import Dense, Flatten
from tensorflow.keras.optimizers import Adam
from tensorflow.keras.preprocessing.image import ImageDataGenerator
```

Figure 15.1 To import necessary libraries.

calculations as in Figure 15.2. The appearance of the red color pop-up notification indicates that Tensorflow has been optimized using the oneDNN package from oneAPI.

In the provided code, a variable named "training_data_dir" is declared, and it is assigned the path to the data directory. The pixel values of the image are normalized by dividing each pixel value as 225. The photos are loaded into the directories training_data_dir and test_data_dir, with the classes "dogs" and "cats" being explicitly defined. A binary class mode is employed, where one class is assigned the label 0 and the other class is assigned the label 1 (see Figure 15.3).

The number of batches in both the training and test sets is determined and subsequently displayed as depicted in Figure 15.4.

15.3 CUSTOM SEQUENTIAL MODEL

The code as given in Figure 15.5 shows an image classification neural network model constructed using the Sequential model from the keras API. The model is composed of convolutional layers that function as feature extractors by applying filters to input images and capturing patterns. Following the convolutions are Max-pooling layers, which reduce spatial dimensions while preserving essential features. The flattened layer converts the multidimensional output into a one-dimensional array, making it suitable for the fully connected layers. Dropout is a regularization technique that deactivates neurons at random during training to prevent overfitting. The final layers consist of densely interconnected (completely interconnected) layers that learn complex patterns and make predictions. Sigmoid activation in the output layer compresses the network's output between 0 and 1, making it suitable for binary classification tasks and indicating the likelihood of an input belonging to a particular class. This architecture, which is commonly employed in image classification tasks, creates a neural network capable of learning intricate patterns from the image data provided.

```
import tensorflow as tf

2023-04-28 05:49:29.938411: I tensorflow/core/platform/cpu_feature_guard.cc:193] This TensorFlow binary is optimized with oneA
PI Deep Neural Network Library (oneDNN) to use the following CPU instructions in performance-critical operations:   AVX2 AVX512
F FMA
To enable them in other operations, rebuild TensorFlow with the appropriate compiler flags.
```

Figure 15.2 Utilizing tensorflow library.

```
# Define the directory containing the training image data for a cat and dog classification task.
training_data_dir = 'cat-and-dog/training_set/training_set'

# Initialize ImageDataGenerator for image preprocessing
datagen = ImageDataGenerator(rescale=1./255)

# Create data generators for training and test sets
training_set = datagen.flow_from_directory(directory=training_data_dir, target_size=(32, 32),
                          classes=['dogs', 'cats'], class_mode='binary', batch_size=20)

# Define test data directory
test_data_dir = 'cat-and-dog/test_set/test_set'
test_set = datagen.flow_from_directory(directory=test_data_dir, target_size=(32, 32),
                          classes=['dogs', 'cats'], class_mode='binary', batch_size=20)
```

```
Found 8006 images belonging to 2 classes.
Found 2023 images belonging to 2 classes.
```

Figure 15.3 Declaring variables and path assignment.

```
# Get the number of batches in the training and test sets
num_batches_training = len(training_set)
num_batches_test = len(test_set)

# Print the number of batches in the training and test sets
print("Number of batches in the training set:", num_batches_training)
print("Number of batches in the test set:", num_batches_test)
```

```
Number of batches in the training set: 401
Number of batches in the test set: 102
```

Figure 15.4 To find batches in the data sets.

We compile the neural network training model. The optimizer, loss function, and metrics are defined as seen from Figure 15.6.

To prevent overfitting during training we implement early stopping with monitor, patience and restore_best_weights as parameters. Then using the fit method, we train the sequential model (refer to Figure 15.7).

15.4 VGG16-BASED MODEL

In this code, a pre-trained VGG16 model without its top classification layers is imported, specifically configured for 32x32 images with three color channels. This model that has been pre-trained is stored in the variable vgg_base. Using the Sequential API, a new neural network model is then constructed. The VGG16 model is incorporated as the foundation of the new model. After the output of VGG16 has been flattened, two custom dense layers with 256 and 128 units, respectively, and ReLU activation functions are added. For binary classification, a dense layer with a single unit and sigmoid activation function is appended. This method leverages the VGG16-learned features while customizing the classification layers for a specific assignment, enabling efficient and effective transfer learning. Refer to Figure 15.8 for the code snippet.

The provided code as in Figure 15.9 entails the compilation of the model using the Adam optimizer, employing a low learning rate, binary crossentropy loss function, and evaluating the model's performance based on accuracy. The technique of early stopping is employed to observe the validation loss during the training process. If the validation loss does not exhibit any improvement for a consecutive period of five epochs, the training is halted. This approach guarantees the preservation of optimal weights. These setups are designed to optimize the training process, hence improving the accuracy of the model and mitigating the risk of overfitting.

```
# Build the neural network model
model = tf.keras.models.Sequential()

model.add(tf.keras.layers.Conv2D(filters=128, kernel_size=3, padding='same', activation='relu', input_shape=[32, 32, 3]))
model.add(tf.keras.layers.MaxPool2D(pool_size=2, strides=2, padding='same'))
model.add(tf.keras.layers.Conv2D(filters=128, kernel_size=3, padding='same', activation='relu'))
model.add(tf.keras.layers.MaxPool2D(pool_size=2, strides=2, padding='same'))
model.add(tf.keras.layers.Flatten())
model.add(tf.keras.layers.Dropout(0.3))
model.add(tf.keras.layers.Dense(units=256, activation='relu'))
model.add(tf.keras.layers.Dense(units=128, activation='relu'))
model.add(tf.keras.layers.Dense(units=1, activation='sigmoid'))
```

Figure 15.5 Building the model.

```
# Compile the model
model.compile(optimizer=tf.keras.optimizers.Adam(learning_rate=0.0001),
              loss='binary_crossentropy',
              metrics=['accuracy'])
```

Figure 15.6 Compiling the model.

Then using the fit method, we train the vgg16 model with several parameters as shown in Figure 15.10.

15.5 ACCURACY COMPARISON

We create two lists models and accuracies to store final end accuracies of all the models used (see Figure 15.11). The accuracies stored in the list show the models' capacity to accurately identify the training data, denoted as percentages.

We use matplotlib to generate a bar graph to compare the levels of accuracy achieved during training by the Sequential model with the VGG16 model as illustrated in Figure 15.12.

15.6 CONCLUSION

Using two very different but equally effective neural network topologies, we have investigated the complexities of picture categorization throughout the course of this chapter. Our investigation has revealed that the Sequential based model performed exceptionally well, highlighting the significance of transfer learning in situations where there is insufficient data. Despite this feat, there is still a large expanse of uncharted possibilities to investigate.

```
# Implement early stopping
early_stopping = tf.keras.callbacks.EarlyStopping(monitor='val_loss', patience=5, restore_best_weights=True)

# Train the model
seq_history = model.fit(
    training_set,
    steps_per_epoch=num_batches_training,
    epochs=10,
    validation_data=test_set,
    validation_steps=num_batches_test,
    callbacks=[early_stopping] # Include early stopping callback
)

Epoch 1/10
401/401 [==============================] - 26s 62ms/step - loss: 0.6640 - accuracy: 0.5891 - val_loss: 0.6127 - val_accuracy: 0.6678
Epoch 2/10
401/401 [==============================] - 17s 41ms/step - loss: 0.5871 - accuracy: 0.6941 - val_loss: 0.5777 - val_accuracy: 0.7044
Epoch 3/10
401/401 [==============================] - 17s 41ms/step - loss: 0.5427 - accuracy: 0.7256 - val_loss: 0.5584 - val_accuracy: 0.7261
Epoch 4/10
401/401 [==============================] - 16s 41ms/step - loss: 0.5036 - accuracy: 0.7584 - val_loss: 0.5268 - val_accuracy: 0.7444
Epoch 5/10
401/401 [==============================] - 16s 41ms/step - loss: 0.4741 - accuracy: 0.7769 - val_loss: 0.5160 - val_accuracy: 0.7523
Epoch 6/10
401/401 [==============================] - 17s 42ms/step - loss: 0.4524 - accuracy: 0.7869 - val_loss: 0.5072 - val_accuracy: 0.7543
Epoch 7/10
401/401 [==============================] - 16s 41ms/step - loss: 0.4256 - accuracy: 0.8048 - val_loss: 0.4969 - val_accuracy: 0.7593
Epoch 8/10
401/401 [==============================] - 17s 42ms/step - loss: 0.4055 - accuracy: 0.8203 - val_loss: 0.4924 - val_accuracy: 0.7682
Epoch 9/10
401/401 [==============================] - 17s 42ms/step - loss: 0.3773 - accuracy: 0.8350 - val_loss: 0.4912 - val_accuracy: 0.7642
Epoch 10/10
401/401 [==============================] - 17s 41ms/step - loss: 0.3570 - accuracy: 0.8405 - val_loss: 0.4941 - val_accuracy: 0.7731
```

Figure 15.7 Training the model.

```
# Load pre-trained VGG16 model without top classification layers (include_top=False)
vgg_base = VGG16(weights='imagenet', include_top=False, input_shape=(32, 32, 3))
# Create a new model on top of the VGG16 base
model = Sequential()
# Add VGG16 base model
model.add(vgg_base)
# Flatten the output of the VGG16 base
model.add(Flatten())
# Add custom dense layers for binary classification
model.add(Dense(units=256, activation='relu'))
model.add(Dense(units=128, activation='relu'))
model.add(Dense(units=1, activation='sigmoid'))
```

Figure 15.8 Constructing the new model.

15.7 FURTHER LEARNING

When we look to the future, there are many different ways to improve the classification models being used for cats and dogs. The models might potentially be fine-tuned to produce even higher performance if intricate hyperparameter configurations are explored as part of the exploration process. It is possible that the models' ability to generalize over a greater variety of real-world events can be improved by enhancing the dataset using a variety of transformations, in addition to utilizing sophisticated techniques such as mixup and cutmix. In addition, looking into more complicated designs such as ResNet, Inception, or EfficientNet might reveal improved feature extraction capabilities.

```
# Compile the model
model.compile(optimizer=Adam(lr=0.0001), loss='binary_crossentropy', metrics=['accuracy'])

WARNING:absl:`lr` is deprecated in Keras optimizer, please use `learning_rate` or use the legacy optimizer, e.g.,tf.keras.optimizers.legacy.Adam.

# Implement early stopping
early_stopping = tf.keras.callbacks.EarlyStopping(monitor='val_loss', patience=5, restore_best_weights=True)
```

Figure 15.9 Compiling the new model with Adam optimizer.

```
# Train the model
vgg16_history = model.fit(
    training_set,
    steps_per_epoch=num_batches_training,
    epochs=10,
    validation_data=test_set,
    validation_steps=num_batches_test,
    callbacks=[early_stopping]
)
```

```
Epoch 1/10
401/401 [==============================] - 93s 229ms/step - loss: 0.7084 - accuracy: 0.4885 - val_loss: 0.6936 - val_accuracy: 0.4998
Epoch 2/10
401/401 [==============================] - 90s 224ms/step - loss: 0.6949 - accuracy: 0.5062 - val_loss: 0.6937 - val_accuracy: 0.5002
Epoch 3/10
401/401 [==============================] - 91s 227ms/step - loss: 0.6951 - accuracy: 0.5074 - val_loss: 0.6934 - val_accuracy: 0.4998
Epoch 4/10
401/401 [==============================] - 90s 225ms/step - loss: 0.6950 - accuracy: 0.5030 - val_loss: 0.6932 - val_accuracy: 0.4998
Epoch 5/10
401/401 [==============================] - 91s 226ms/step - loss: 0.6933 - accuracy: 0.4973 - val_loss: 0.6931 - val_accuracy: 0.4998
Epoch 6/10
401/401 [==============================] - 90s 224ms/step - loss: 0.6932 - accuracy: 0.4975 - val_loss: 0.6931 - val_accuracy: 0.5002
Epoch 7/10
401/401 [==============================] - 91s 227ms/step - loss: 0.6932 - accuracy: 0.4835 - val_loss: 0.6931 - val_accuracy: 0.5002
Epoch 8/10
401/401 [==============================] - 90s 224ms/step - loss: 0.6932 - accuracy: 0.4908 - val_loss: 0.6931 - val_accuracy: 0.5002
Epoch 9/10
401/401 [==============================] - 91s 227ms/step - loss: 0.6932 - accuracy: 0.4985 - val_loss: 0.6931 - val_accuracy: 0.5002
Epoch 10/10
401/401 [==============================] - 90s 224ms/step - loss: 0.6932 - accuracy: 0.4933 - val_loss: 0.6931 - val_accuracy: 0.5002
```

Figure 15.10 Training the vgg16 model.

```
# Plotting the accuracy comparison using a bar graph
models = ['Sequential Model', 'VGG16 Model']
accuracies = [seq_history.history['accuracy'][-1] * 100, vgg16_history.history['accuracy'][-1] * 100]
```

Figure 15.11 For plotting Accuracy comparison.

```
plt.figure(figsize=(8, 6))
plt.bar(models, accuracies, color=['blue', 'green'])
plt.ylabel('Accuracy (%)')
plt.title('Accuracy Comparison: Sequential vs. VGG16')
plt.ylim(0, 100)

# Display the accuracy values on the bars
for index, value in enumerate(accuracies):
    plt.text(index, value + 2, str(round(value, 2)) + '%', ha='center', va='bottom', fontsize=12)

plt.show()
```

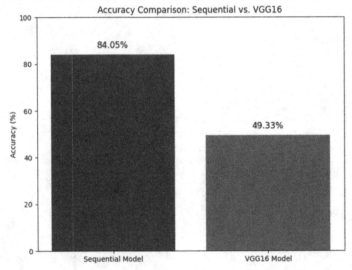

Figure 15.12 Accuracy comparison.

Chapter 16

Maximizing placement predictions with outlier removal

LEARNING OBJECTIVES

After concluding this chapter, the reader shall be able to:

- Explore the student placement details with machine learning techniques.
- Familiarize themselves with predictive modeling.

16.1 INTRODUCTION

Data-driven decision-making is essential for achieving success in the ever-changing realm of college recruitment. This chapter aims to explore the intricacies of student placement through the utilization of machine learning techniques. The analysis is conducted based on the Kaggle Campus Recruitment dataset: www.kaggle.com/datasets/benroshan/factors-affecting-campus-placement/, which provides valuable insights into this domain. By employing a systematic methodology for data preprocessing and including novel methods for outlier detection and elimination, we delve into the core of predictive modeling. The notion is to provide educational institutions and recruiters with the necessary resources to make well-informed and strategic judgments regarding placements.

16.2 DATA PREPROCESSING AND SPLITTING

We are incorporating fundamental libraries that serve as the foundation for our data analysis and machine learning pursuits as witnessed in Figure 16.1. The libraries numpy and pandas are imported to handle data. The seaborn and matplotlib libraries are used for data visualization tasks. From the sklearn library we import the necessary models needed.

We import our dataset and store it in a variable named "df." We have a clear look at the first five rows of our imported dataset using the. head() command. It's evident that our dataset has both numerical and string values

DOI: 10.1201/9781032676685-17

```
[1]  import numpy as np
     import pandas as pd
     import seaborn as sns
     import matplotlib.pyplot as plt
     from sklearn.model_selection import train_test_split
     from sklearn.ensemble import RandomForestClassifier
     from sklearn.svm import SVC
     from sklearn.linear_model import LogisticRegression
     from sklearn.metrics import accuracy_score
     from sklearn.preprocessing import LabelEncoder
     from scipy import stats
```

Figure 16.1 To import necessary libraries.

which will be handled in further pre-processing steps. Refer to Figure 16.2 for the details.

As we move forward let's look at the number of missing values using isnull().sum() command as provided in Figure 16.3. As we have the result with us, we have 67 missing values in the salary column so let's find a method to fill this.

Here we fill the null values in the salary column. First, we access the salary column in the df Dataframe then using the fillna method we fill the NaN values in the salary column by median of non-missing values in the same column. Refer to Figure 16.4 for the code snippet.

As we discussed previously, the dataframe consists of both numeric and categorical values so let's now replace all the string values. Initially, we create an empty dictionary to store label encoder all the instances for each categorical column. Then we iterate through all the columns and find out the columns having object values. A labelencoder() object is created to encode all the categorical values in the dataframe. Using the .head() command we can see all our columns are numeric now. See Figure 16.5.

Then we create the training and testing set. For this we first create a variable called features where we drop the target variable "status" and store all the features. Then we store our target column "status" in labels variable. Then using the train test split method we split the dataset into 80% of the data for Training and 20% for Testing as depicted in Figure 16.6.

16.4 OUTLIER REMOVAL USING Z-SCORE

Outliers can be defined as data points that exhibit substantial deviation from the prevailing pattern observed within the sample. Instances of these phenomena may manifest as a result of a multitude of circumstances, including inaccuracies in data collecting, variations in measurement precision, or the

```
# load the dataset
df = pd.read_csv('/content/Placement_Data_Full_Class.csv')
```

```
df.head()
```

sl_no	gender	ssc_p	ssc_b	hsc_p	hsc_b	hsc_s	degree_p	degree_t	workex	etest_p	specialisation	mba_p	status	salary
0	1	M	67.00	Others	91.00	Others	Commerce	58.00	Sci&Tech	No	55.0	Mkt&HR	58.80	Placed	270000.0
1	2	M	79.33	Central	78.33	Others	Science	77.48	Sci&Tech	Yes	86.5	Mkt&Fin	66.28	Placed	200000.0
2	3	M	65.00	Central	68.00	Central	Arts	64.00	Comm&Mgmt	No	75.0	Mkt&Fin	57.80	Placed	250000.0
3	4	M	56.00	Central	52.00	Central	Science	52.00	Sci&Tech	No	66.0	Mkt&HR	59.43	Not Placed	NaN
4	5	M	85.80	Central	73.60	Central	Commerce	73.30	Comm&Mgmt	No	96.8	Mkt&Fin	55.50	Placed	425000.0

Figure 16.2 Code snippet to load the dataset.

```
df.isnull().sum()
```

```
sl_no             0
gender            0
ssc_p             0
ssc_b             0
hsc_p             0
hsc_b             0
hsc_s             0
degree_p          0
degree_t          0
workex            0
etest_p           0
specialisation    0
mba_p             0
status            0
salary            67
dtype: int64
```

Figure 16.3 To find the missing values.

```
[5]   # Handling missing values in the 'salary' column
      df['salary'] = df['salary'].fillna(df['salary'].median())
```

Figure 16.4 Filling the null values.

occurrence of genuinely infrequent events. Although outliers can occasionally signify intriguing events, they can also inject extraneous data into our analysis, resulting in deceptive interpretations and forecasts. The Z-score, alternatively referred to as the standard score, holds significant importance as a fundamental statistical measure within the field of data analysis. The measure quantifies the number of standard deviations by which a given data point deviates from the mean of the dataset. By doing Z-score calculations on each data point, it is possible to detect values that deviate significantly from the mean and are likely to be considered outliers.

```
[6] # Encode categorical features using LabelEncoder
    label_encoders = {}
    for col in df.select_dtypes(include=['object']).columns:
        label_encoders[col] = LabelEncoder()
        df[col] = label_encoders[col].fit_transform(df[col])
```

df.head()

	sl_no	gender	ssc_p	ssc_b	hsc_p	hsc_b	hsc_s	degree_p	degree_t	workex	etest_p	specialisation	mba_p	status	salary
0	1	1	67.00	1	91.00	1	1	58.00	2	0	55.0	1	58.80	1	270000.0
1	2	1	79.33	0	78.33	1	2	77.48	2	1	86.5	0	66.28	1	200000.0
2	3	1	65.00	0	68.00	0	0	64.00	0	0	75.0	0	57.80	1	250000.0
3	4	1	56.00	0	52.00	0	2	52.00	2	0	66.0	1	59.43	0	265000.0
4	5	1	85.80	0	73.60	0	1	73.30	0	0	96.8	0	55.50	1	425000.0

Figure 16.5 To encode values.

```
[7] # Split the data into features (X) and labels (y)
    features = df.drop('status', axis=1)
    labels = df['status']

    # Split the data into training and test sets
    features_train, features_test, labels_train, labels_test = train_test_split(features, labels, test_size=0.2, random_state=0)
```

Figure 16.6 Splitting the dataset.

```
[8] # Detect and remove outliers using Z-score method
    selected_columns = ['hsc_p', 'degree_p', 'salary']
    z_scores = np.abs(stats.zscore(features_train[selected_columns]))
    threshold = 3
    outlier_indices = np.where(z_scores > threshold)[0]
    features_train = features_train.drop(features_train.index[outlier_indices])
    labels_train = labels_train.drop(labels_train.index[outlier_indices])
```

Figure 16.7 To detect and remove outliers.

In columns "hsc_p," "degree_p," and "salary" we calculate the Z-scores and compare it with a defined threshold which is three in our case to identify and remove the outliers. Refer to Figure 16.7 for the code snippet.

16.4 MODELING

Three distinct machine learning classifiers are instantiated, appended to a list along with their respective names, and a dictionary is established to record accuracy scores as provided in Figure 16.8.

```
# Initialize classifiers
random_forest = RandomForestClassifier(random_state=0, class_weight='balanced')
svm_classifier = SVC(random_state=0, class_weight='balanced', probability=True)
logistic_regression = LogisticRegression(random_state=0, class_weight='balanced')

# List of classifiers and their names
classifiers = [(random_forest, 'Random Forest'), (svm_classifier, 'SVM'), (logistic_regression, 'Logistic Regression')]

# Dictionary to store accuracy scores
accuracy_scores = {}
```

Figure 16.8 Classifiers instantiation.

```
[10]  # Train and evaluate each model
      for clf, clf_name in classifiers:
          clf.fit(features_train, labels_train)
          accuracy = clf.score(features_test, labels_test)
          accuracy_scores[clf_name] = accuracy

      # Print accuracy scores
      for clf_name, accuracy in accuracy_scores.items():
          print(f'{clf_name} Accuracy: {round(accuracy * 100, 2)}%')
```

```
Random Forest Accuracy: 86.05%
SVM Accuracy: 39.53%
Logistic Regression Accuracy: 67.44%
```

Figure 16.9 Model training and evaluation.

We train three different classifiers with our training data. We create a loop to iterate through the list containing the tuple of classifier objects which we created during the previous step. Then we fit the training data separated to the created models and calculate the accuracy using the test labels after we train the model. At last we print the accuracy of all the three models and the codes used is given in Figure 16.9.

16.5 MODEL COMPARISON AND VISUALIZATION

A bar graph is created as seen in Figure 16.10 to compare the accuracy scores of the three different machine learning models.

```
# Plotting bar graph to compare accuracy
plt.figure(figsize=(8, 6))
plt.bar(accuracy_scores.keys(), accuracy_scores.values(), color=['blue', 'orange', 'green'])
plt.ylabel('Accuracy')
plt.title('Model Accuracy Comparison')
plt.ylim(0, 1)
plt.xticks(rotation=15)
plt.tight_layout()
plt.show()
```

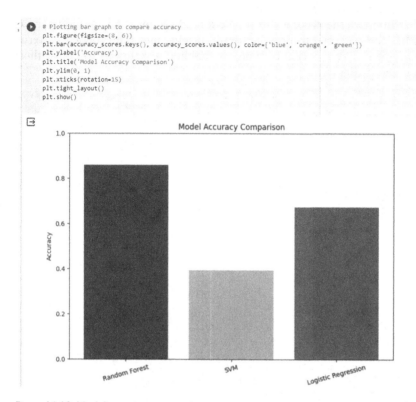

Figure 16.10 Model accuracy comparison.

16.6 CONCLUSION

In the context of campus recruitment, the foundation for effective placements is reliant on precise prognostications. The present comparative investigation sheds light on the trajectory forward, elucidating the merits and limitations of diverse machine learning algorithms. The Random Forest model emerges as the leading candidate, exhibiting a notable accuracy rate of 86.05%. This chapter offers insights into the realm of predictive modeling and empowers decision-makers with the necessary information to make informed decisions based on data in the recruitment process.

16.7 FURTHER LEARNING

As we conclude this chapter, it is imperative to recognize the extensive range of opportunities that awaits in the future. Potential areas for future investigation include the exploration of ensemble techniques, the application of feature engineering, and the examination of deep learning methodologies to further improve the accuracy of predictions. Moreover, a longitudinal analysis has the potential to provide useful insights into the evolving patterns of placement over a period of time, so enabling institutions to adjust their policies accordingly.

Chapter 17

A deep dive into Mushroom classification with oneAPI

LEARNING OBJECTIVES

After reading this chapter, the reader shall be able to:

- Acquire the knowledge to classify mushrooms through machine learning techniques.
- Utilize diverse machine learning algorithms to achieve high accuracy.

17.1 INTRODUCTION

This chapter initiates an engaging exploration into the domain of machine learning, with the Mushroom classification dataset sourced from Kaggle, www.kaggle.com/datasets/uciml/mushroom-classification/data, as the primary reference. The information presented in the dataset encompasses a wide range of characteristics pertaining to mushrooms, hence inciting our inquisitiveness to delve into the realm of mycology from the perspective of data science and artificial intelligence. Through the utilization of diverse machine learning algorithms, our objective is to comprehend the intricacies involved in the classification of mushrooms, specifically distinguishing between edible and deadly types with a high level of accuracy.

17.2 DATA PREPROCESSING AND SPLITTING

To start with, we import several necessary libraries as presented in Figure 17.1. We import pandas and numpy to handle and manipulate data. We have done an extensive exploratory data analysis to import seaborn and matplotlib library. For modeling we import all the ML algorithms from the scikit-learn library. We have optimized all the machine learning models using Intel's oneAPI tool and we have used some custom library for patching scikit-learn. The red colored pop-up message tells us that the environment is optimized with oneAPI.

DOI: 10.1201/9781032676685-18

```
import numpy as np # Linear algebra
import pandas as pd # data processing, CSV file I/O (e.g. pd.read_csv)
import matplotlib.pyplot as plt
import seaborn as sns
from sklearnex import patch_sklearn
patch_sklearn()
import numpy as np
import pandas as pd
from sklearn.model_selection import train_test_split
from sklearn.metrics import accuracy_score, classification_report
from sklearn.datasets import load_iris
from sklearn.linear_model import LogisticRegression
from sklearn.tree import DecisionTreeClassifier
from sklearn.ensemble import RandomForestClassifier, AdaBoostClassifier, GradientBoostingClassifier
from sklearn.svm import SVC
from sklearn.neighbors import KNeighborsClassifier
from sklearn.naive_bayes import GaussianNB
from sklearn.neural_network import MLPClassifier
from sklearn.discriminant_analysis import LinearDiscriminantAnalysis, QuadraticDiscriminantAnalysis
Intel(R) Extension for Scikit-learn* enabled (https://github.com/intel/scikit-learn-intelex)
```

Figure 17.1 Importing the libraries.

```
# Load the dataset (assuming 'data' is your dataset variable)
data = pd.read_csv('mushrooms.csv')

data.head()
```

	class	cap-shape	cap-surface	cap-color	bruises	odor	gill-attachment	gill-spacing	gill-size	gill-color	...
0	p	x	s	n	t	p	f	c	n	k	...
1	e	x	s	y	t	a	f	c	b	k	...
2	e	b	s	w	t	l	f	c	b	n	...
3	p	x	y	w	t	p	f	c	n	n	...
4	e	x	s	g	f	n	f	w	b	k	...

5 rows × 23 columns

Figure 17.2 Code snippet to import the dataset.

We then import the dataset and store it into a variable called data using the read_csv command then we have a look at the first five rows of our dataset as seen in Figure 17.2. All the columns in our dataset are categorical so let us perform encoding in further steps.

We check the dataset for null values; it is clear that no null values are present in our dataset as seen from the result of Figure 17.3.

As already discussed, we have to convert all the categorical values available in our dataset to numeric. We use the LabelEncoder to convert categorical into numeric and the resultant data frame is stored in the variable data_encoded. See Figure 17.4.

17.3 EXPLORATORY DATA ANALYSIS

In this section, we create various visualizations to understand the data better.

First, we create a pie chart to understand our target column "class" better. We have two unique values e and p in the column. We use the .value_counts() command to count both the unique values and the results are stored and displayed. The code snippet of the same is provided in Figure 17.5.

The red portion of Figure 17.6 corresponds to the proportion of poisonous mushrooms present in the dataset. The portion denoted in light blue is the proportion of edible mushrooms. The proportions of these classes are relatively comparable.

We move on to check and analyze specific important columns in our dataset. Start with the "cap-shape" column and count the unique values that are sorted in descending values based on their occurrence time. Then the value counts are visualized with a barplot (Streit and Gehlenborg, 2014). It

```
[4]:  data.isnull().sum()
```

```
[4]:  class                       0
      cap-shape                   0
      cap-surface                 0
      cap-color                   0
      bruises                     0
      odor                        0
      gill-attachment             0
      gill-spacing                0
      gill-size                   0
      gill-color                  0
      stalk-shape                 0
      stalk-root                  0
      stalk-surface-above-ring    0
      stalk-surface-below-ring    0
      stalk-color-above-ring      0
      stalk-color-below-ring      0
      veil-type                   0
      veil-color                  0
      ring-number                 0
      ring-type                   0
      spore-print-color           0
      population                  0
      habitat                     0
      dtype: int64
```

Figure 17.3 Check for null values in the dataset.

is clear that type X has the highest count and c has the lowest count among all, as evident from Figure 17.7.

Once after importing the necessary libraries the figure size is set to 15 x 8 inches, a countplot is generated as in Figure 17.8 with seaborn in which the x-axis represents the cap-shape and hue is class. Custom colors are assigned to represent "Poisonous" and "Edible" classes.

From the graph of Figure 17.9, the convex shaped cap has more poisonous as well as edible mushrooms followed by flat shaped mushrooms.

The same method is followed to create a plot but the minor difference is in the distribution of mushrooms that are categorized by their classes and

```
[5]: from sklearn.preprocessing import LabelEncoder

     data_encoded = data.copy()
     le = LabelEncoder()
     for col in data_encoded.columns:
         data_encoded[col] = le.fit_transform(data_encoded[col])

     data_encoded.head()
```

[5]:

	class	cap-shape	cap-surface	cap-color	bruises	odor	gill-attachment	gill-spacing	gill-size	gill-color	...	stalk-surface-below-ring	stalk-color-above-ring	stalk-color-below-ring	veil-type	veil-color	ring-number	ring-type	spore-print-color	population
0	1	5	2	4	1	6	1	0	1	4	...	2	7	7	0	2	1	4	2	3
1	0	5	2	9	1	0	1	0	0	4	...	2	7	7	0	2	1	4	3	2
2	2	0	2	8	1	3	1	0	0	5	...	2	7	7	0	2	1	4	3	2
3	1	5	3	8	1	6	1	0	1	5	...	2	7	7	0	2	1	4	2	3
4	0	5	2	3	0	5	1	1	0	4	...	2	7	7	0	2	1	0	3	0

5 rows × 23 columns

Figure 17.4 Using LabelEncoder.

```
[6]:  target_column = "class"
      value_counts = data[target_column].value_counts()
      print(value_counts)

      class
      e     4208
      p     3916
      Name: count, dtype: int64
```

Figure 17.5 To count the unique values.

habitats, with all the specified customizations. Refer to Figure 17.10 for the code snippet.

From Figure 17.11, it is evident that Woods is a great habitat whereas Waste is a bad habitat for mushrooms to be grown.

17.4 MODELING AND COMPARISON

Now we move on to the modeling step for that. Initially we split our dataset into a testing and training set. All the features present in our dataframe are assigned to a variable called X and the target is stored in y. Then, using the train_test_split module, we split our dataset to 80% training and 20% testing set as illustrated in Figure 17.12.

Several ML models are trained and evaluated with the testing data and the accuracy of all these models is printed down in the console. See Figure 17.13.

A dictionary, model_accuracies is created as in Figure 17.14 and the calculated accuracy scores using the accuracy_score function is stored in it.

The above code as in Figure 17.15 generates a bar plot which represents the accuracy of different models.

The Support Vector Machine model performs best with 99% accuracy, closely followed by Logistic Regression on a par with Linear Discriminant Analysis with 95% accuracy, while Naive Bayes performs last with 92% accuracy as seen from Figure 17.16.

17.5 CONCLUSION

This chapter has delved into the intriguing domain of mushroom classification through the implementation of machine learning methodologies. By employing preprocessing, visualization, and model training techniques, we have distinguished effectively and precisely between poisonous and palatable mushrooms. Our investigation serves to augment our comprehension

```
•[7]:  import matplotlib.pyplot as plt
       # Pie chart, where the slices will be ordered and plotted counter-clockwise:
       labels = value_counts.index
       sizes = value_counts.values
       colors = ['lightblue', 'lightcoral']  # Define colors for the slices
       explode = (0.1, 0)  #"explode" the 1st slice (i.e., 'explode' the 1st val
       plt.pie(sizes, explode=explode, labels=labels, colors=colors, autopct='%1.1f%%', shadow=True, startangle=140)
       plt.axis('equal')  # Equal aspect ratio ensures that pie is drawn as a circle.
       # Add a title
       plt.title("Distribution of Target Values")
       # Display the pie chart
       plt.show()
```

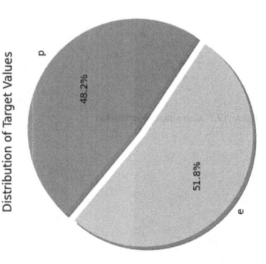

Distribution of Target Values

Figure 17.6 Target value distribution.

```
•[8]:  import pandas as pd
       import matplotlib.pyplot as plt
       cap_shape_column = "cap-shape"  # Replace with the actual column name
       # Count the unique values in the "cap_shape" column and sort them by value counts in descending order:
       value_counts = data[cap_shape_column].value_counts().sort_values(ascending=False)
       # Create a bar plot:
       plt.figure(figsize=(8, 6))
       value_counts.plot(kind='bar', color='lightblue')
       # Customize the plot
       plt.title("Distribution of Cap Shapes")
       plt.xlabel("Cap Shape")
       plt.ylabel("Count")
       # Display the bar plot
       plt.show()
```

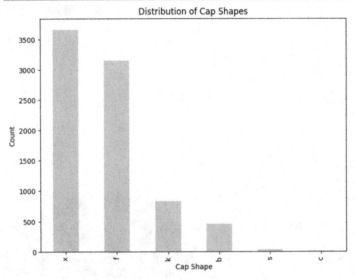

Figure 17.7 Cap shape distribution.

```
[9]:   import pandas as pd
       import seaborn as sns
       import matplotlib.pyplot as plt
       # Create a Seaborn countplot with customizations:
       plt.figure(figsize=(15, 8))
       splot = sns.countplot(data=data, x='cap-shape',
                             hue='class',
                             order=data['cap-shape'].value_counts().index,
                             palette=['lightcoral', 'lightgreen'],
                             edgecolor=(0, 0, 0),
                             linewidth=2)

       # Set custom x-tick labels
       splot.set_xticklabels(['Convex', 'Flat', 'Knobbed', 'Bell', 'Sunken', 'Conical'])
       # Annotate the bars with their counts
       for p in splot.patches:
           splot.annotate(format(p.get_height(), '.1f'),
                          (p.get_x() + p.get_width() / 2., p.get_height()),
                          ha='center', va='center',
                          xytext=(0, 9),
                          textcoords='offset points')

       # Customize the legend, labels, and title
       plt.legend(['Poisonous', 'Edible'], loc='upper right')
       plt.ylabel('Number of Mushrooms', fontsize=14)
       plt.xlabel('Types of Cap Shapes of Mushrooms', fontsize=14)
       plt.xticks(fontsize=12)
       plt.yticks(fontsize=12)
       plt.title('Distribution of Mushrooms by Classes and Cap Shapes', fontsize=20)
       # Display the plot
       plt.show()
```

Figure 17.8 Generating a countplot.

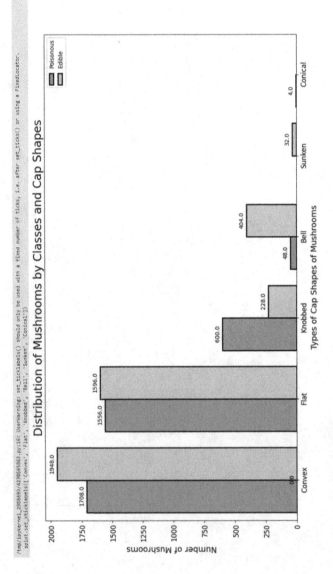

Figure 17.9 Distribution Types.

```
[10]:  plt.figure(figsize=(15, 8))
       splot = sns.countplot(data=data, x='habitat',
                            hue='class',
                            order=data['habitat'].value_counts().index,
                            palette=['lightcoral', 'lightgreen'],
                            edgecolor=(0, 0, 0),
                            linewidth=2)

       splot.set_xticklabels(['Woods', 'Grasses', 'Paths', 'Leaves', 'Urban', 'Meadows', 'Waste'])

       for p in splot.patches:
           splot.annotate(format(p.get_height(), '.1f'),
                          (p.get_x() + p.get_width() / 2., p.get_height()),
                          ha='center', va='center',
                          xytext=(0, 9),
                          textcoords='offset points')

       plt.legend(['Poisonous', 'Edible'], loc='upper right')
       plt.ylabel('Number of the Mushrooms', fontsize=14)
       plt.xlabel('Habitats', fontsize=14)
       plt.xticks(fontsize=12)
       plt.yticks(fontsize=12)
       plt.title('Distribution of the Mushrooms by their Classes vs Habitats', fontsize=20)
```

Figure 17.10 Creating a Plot.

/tmp/ipykernel_2988693/2285874222.py:9: UserWarning: set_ticklabels() should only be used with a fixed number of ticks, i.e. after set_ticks() or using a FixedLocator.
  splot.set_xticklabels(['Woods', 'Grasses', 'Paths', 'Leaves', 'Urban', 'Meadows', 'Waste'])

[30]: Text(0.5, 1.0, 'Distribution of the Mushrooms by their Classes vs Habitats')

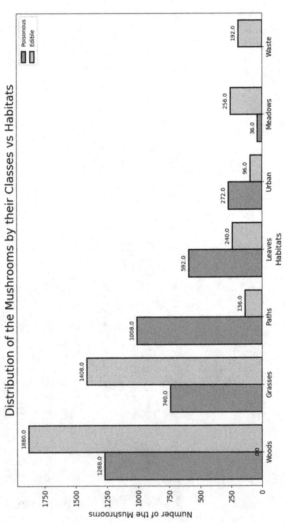

Figure 17.11 Distribution by habitat.

```
[11]:  y = data_encoded[['class']]     # The label for the machine learning models
       X = data_encoded.drop(['class'], axis=1)    #Features
```

```
[12]:  from sklearn.model_selection import train_test_split
       X_train, X_test, y_train, y_test = train_test_split(X, y, test_size=0.2, random_state=42)
```

Figure 17.12 Dataset splitting.

```
[14]: models = {
          "Logistic Regression": LogisticRegression(),
          "Support Vector Machine": SVC(),
          "Naive Bayes": GaussianNB(),
          "Linear Discriminant Analysis": LinearDiscriminantAnalysis(),
      }

      for model_name, model in models.items():
          model.fit(X_train, y_train)
          y_pred = model.predict(X_test)
          accuracy = accuracy_score(y_test, y_pred)
          print(f"Model: {model_name}")
          print("Accuracy: ", accuracy)
          print("\n")
```

```
Model: Logistic Regression
Accuracy:  0.947076923076923


Model: Support Vector Machine
Accuracy:  0.9926153846153846


Model: Naive Bayes
Accuracy:  0.9218461538461539
```

Figure 17.13 Model training and evaluation.

```
[15]: model_accuracies = {}
      for model_name, model in models.items():
          model.fit(X_train, y_train)
          y_pred = model.predict(X_test)
          accuracy = accuracy_score(y_test, y_pred)
          model_accuracies[model_name] = accuracy
```

Figure 17.14 Using accuracy_score function.

```
import matplotlib.pyplot as plt
# Extract model names and their corresponding accuracies
model_names = list(model_accuracies.keys())
accuracies = list(model_accuracies.values())
# Create a bar plot
plt.figure(figsize=(12, 6))
bars = plt.bar(model_names, accuracies, color='gold',linewidth=2)
plt.xlabel('Machine Learning Models', fontsize=14)
plt.ylabel('Accuracy', fontsize=14)
plt.title('Model Comparison', fontsize=16)
plt.xticks(rotation=45, fontsize=12)
plt.yticks(fontsize=12)
plt.ylim(0, 1) # Set the y-axis limits to the range of accuracy (0 to 1)
# Add accuracy values on top of the bars
for bar, accuracy in zip(bars, accuracies):
    plt.text(bar.get_x() + bar.get_width() / 2 - 0.1, bar.get_height() + 0.01, f'{accuracy:.2f}', fontsize=12, color='black')
plt.show()
```

Figure 17.15 Bar plot generation.

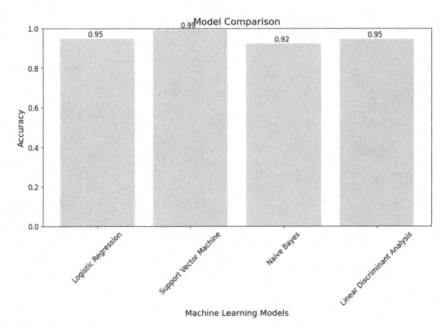

Figure 17.16 Model comparison.

of fungi while also highlighting the efficacy of machine learning in resolving complex practical challenges.

17.6 FURTHER LEARNING

Although our models have achieved noteworthy outcomes so far, the expedition remains ongoing. Subsequent pursuits may entail investigating novel methodologies, such as neural networks, in an effort to improve the precision of our categorizations. Furthermore, by expanding the datasets and investigating various deep learning architectures, it may be possible to discern particular mushroom species, thereby creating novel opportunities for further investigation and practical implementation.

SUGGESTED READING

Streit, M. and Gehlenborg, N., 2014. Bar charts and box plots: Creating a simple yet effective plot requires an understanding of data and tasks. *Nature Methods*, *11*(2), pp.117–118.

## Chapter 18

Smart healthcare

Machine learning approaches for kidney disease prediction with oneAPI

LEARNING OBJECTIVES

After reading this chapter, the reader shall be able to:

- Acquire the knowledge to classify kidney disease through machine learning techniques.
- Utilize diverse machine learning algorithms to accomplish enhanced diagnostic accuracy.

18.1 INTRODUCTION

The term "chronic kidney disease" refers to a disorder that affects a significant portion of the population and is defined by a steady loss of kidney function. It is essential to an effective management strategy to detect CKD in its earlier stages when it is still treatable. The Kaggle Chronic Kidney Disease dataset with the link given is used throughout this chapter as a basis for our classification of CKD using the capabilities of the machine learning: www.kaggle.com/datasets/mansoordaku/ckdisease. We hope to make a substantial contribution to the area of healthcare by greatly improving the diagnostic accuracy of chronic kidney disease (CKD) through the application of cutting-edge algorithms and data preparation strategies.

18.2 DATA PREPROCESSING AND SPLITTING

We first import the necessary libraries for data visualization, data manipulation, and model building. The red colored pop-up, as shown in Figure 18.1, tells us the whole code is optimized with oneAPI.

We then import our dataset into the kernel and store it in a variable called data, and look at the first five rows of our imported dataset. It is clear from the inference that we have a mix of both numeric and categorical values, which will be taken care of in the further steps (see Figure 18.2). We can also notice the presence of NaN (Not A Number) values (Chandradas, A., 2021)

DOI: 10.1201/9781032676685-19

```
[1]: # Importing the necessary libraries
     import pandas as pd
     import numpy as np
     import matplotlib.pyplot as pltz
     from sklearn.model_selection import train_test_split

     Intel(R) Extension for Scikit-learn* enabled (https://github.com/intel/scikit-learn-intelex)
```

Figure 18.1 Importing the required libraries.

```
data=pd.read_csv("kidney_disease.csv")

data.head(5)
```

	id	age	bp	sg	al	su	rbc	pc	pcc	ba	...
0	0	48.0	80.0	1.020	1.0	0.0	NaN	normal	notpresent	notpresent	...
1	1	7.0	50.0	1.020	4.0	0.0	NaN	normal	notpresent	notpresent	...
2	2	62.0	80.0	1.010	2.0	3.0	normal	normal	notpresent	notpresent	...
3	3	48.0	70.0	1.005	4.0	0.0	normal	abnormal	present	notpresent	...
4	4	51.0	80.0	1.010	2.0	0.0	normal	normal	notpresent	notpresent	...

5 rows × 26 columns

Figure 18.2 To import the dataset.

in some columns and the column ID seems irrelevant for finding our target variable. The Classification column is our target column.

As discussed in the previous step, we will drop the ID column from our dataset using the drop function. Then we see the short summary of our data frame using the info() function as seen in Figure 18.3.

We look at the unique values in each column of our dataset using the unique() function as shown in Figure 18.4. We check for mis-entered values in our dataset. Here we can see 43 is mistyped as "\t43." We manually check and change all the values in the next step.

We use the replace() function and manually map the correct variables to the corresponding mistyped wrong variables which are found in the previous step. The replaced dataset is again stored in a duplicate variable called data (see Figure 18.5).

In the first step, upon looking at our dataset initially we find some missing values. We use the isnull().sum() command to look at the null values in our dataset and yes, we have missing values in almost all the columns (see Figure 18.6).

In this step, we create two variables num_cols where we store all the columns with numeric values and cat_cols with categorical columns. All these columns have some amount of missing values, which we will be replacing with two different methods. For the numeric columns we use the mean() method; that is, we calculate the mean value of a particular column and fill all the null values in the column. Similarly for the categorical column we use the backfill method in which we fill each of the null values with the next valid value in the column. See Figure 18.7 for the code snippet.

```
[4]:  # dropping id column
      data.drop('id', axis = 1, inplace = True)
```

```
[5]:  data.info()
      <class 'pandas.core.frame.DataFrame'>
      RangeIndex: 400 entries, 0 to 399
      Data columns (total 25 columns):
       #   Column          Non-Null Count   Dtype
      ---  ------          --------------   -----
       0   age             391 non-null     float64
       1   bp              388 non-null     float64
       2   sg              353 non-null     float64
       3   al              354 non-null     float64
       4   su              351 non-null     float64
       5   rbc             248 non-null     object
       6   pc  .           335 non-null     object
       7   pcc             396 non-null     object
       8   ba              396 non-null     object
       9   bgr             356 non-null     float64
       10  bu              381 non-null     float64
       11  sc              383 non-null     float64
       12  sod             313 non-null     float64
       13  pot             312 non-null     float64
       14  hemo            348 non-null     float64
       15  pcv             330 non-null     object
       16  wc              295 non-null     object
       17  rc              270 non-null     object
       18  htn             398 non-null     object
       19  dm              398 non-null     object
       20  cad             398 non-null     object
       21  appet           399 non-null     object
       22  pe              399 non-null     object
       23  ane             399 non-null     object
       24  classification  400 non-null     object
      dtypes: float64(11), object(14)
      memory usage: 78.2+ KB
```

Figure 18.3 Using drop and info function.

After filling the null values as in Figure 18.8, we again look at the result.

Let us first encode the categorical variables present in our dataset to numeric using the LabelEncoder method as shown in Figure 18.9. A variable cat_cols is created in which a list containing the names of all categorical columns from our dataset is stored. Then, using the label encoder method,

```
[6]: print(data['rbc'].unique())
     print("############################")
     print(data['pc'].unique())
     print("############################")
     print(data['pcc'].unique())
     print("############################")
     print(data['ba'].unique())
     print("############################")
     print(data['pcv'].unique())
     print("############################")
     print(data['wc'].unique())
     print("############################")
     print(data['rc'].unique())
     print("############################")
     print(data['htn'].unique())
     print("############################")
     print(data['dm'].unique())
     print("############################")
     print(data['cad'].unique())
     print("############################")
     print(data['appet'].unique())
     print("############################")
     print(data['pe'].unique())
     print("############################")
     print(data['ane'].unique())
     print("############################")
     print(data['classification'].unique())
```

```
[nan 'normal' 'abnormal']
############################
['normal' 'abnormal' nan]
############################
['notpresent' 'present' nan]
############################
['notpresent' 'present' nan]
############################
['44' '38' '31' '32' '35' '39' '36' '33' '29' '28' nan '16' '24' '37' '30'
 '34' '40' '45' '27' '48' '\t?' '52' '14' '22' '18' '42' '17' '46' '23'
 '19' '25' '41' '26' '15' '21' '43' '20' '\t43' '47' '9' '49' '50' '53'
 '51' '54']
```

Figure 18.4 Using unique function.

each column is converted to numerical values making it suitable for machine learning algorithms.

Our dataset contains only numerical values now after encoding all the categorical columns and all the null values have been filled. The same can be seen in Figure 18.10.

18.3 MODELING

Then we import the necessary libraries as represented in Figure 18.11 to create our models. For splitting the data into training and testing sets we

```
#Dealing with abnormally values:
data=data.replace({'\t':np.nan , '\t43':43, '\t6200':6200 , '\t8400':8400, '\t?':np.nan, 'ckd\t':'ckd","'tyes":'yes","\tno':'no", 'yes":'yes"})

print(data['rbc'].unique())
print("###################################")
print(data['pc'].unique())
print("###################################")
print(data['pcc'].unique())
print("###################################")
print(data['ba'].unique())
print("###################################")
print(data['pcv'].unique())
print("###################################")
print(data['wc'].unique())
print("###################################")
print(data['rc'].unique())
print("###################################")
print(data['htn'].unique())
print("###################################")
print(data['dm'].unique())
print("###################################")
print(data['cad'].unique())
print("###################################")
print(data['appet'].unique())
print("###################################")
print(data['pe'].unique())
print("###################################")
print(data['ane'].unique())
print("###################################")
print(data['classification'].unique())

[nan 'normal' 'abnormal']
###################################
['normal' 'abnormal' nan]
###################################
['notpresent' 'present' nan]
###################################
['notpresent' 'present' nan]
```

Figure 18.5 Using replace function.

```
[9]: data.isnull().sum()

[9]: age                  9
     bp                  12
     sg                  47
     al                  46
     su                  49
     rbc                152
     pc                  65
     pcc                  4
     ba                   4
     bgr                 44
     bu                  19
     sc                  17
     sod                 87
     pot                 88
     hemo                52
     pcv                 71
     wc                 106
     rc                 131
     htn                  2
     dm                   2
     cad                  2
     appet                1
     pe                   1
     ane                  1
     classification       0
     dtype: int64
```

Figure 18.6 To find the missing values.

first create two variables, X and y. In the variable X, we store all the features by dropping the target column classification. In y we store only the classification column. Then we split our data into a Training and testing set which is 80% and 20% respectively.

The logistic regression (LR) classifier is initialized first as seen from Figure 18.12. Then we fit our training data to train our initialized logistic regression model. The predict function is used to make predictions on the test data.

Here the SVM classifier is initialized and trained as depicted in Figure 18.13.

Here the KNN classifier is initialized and trained as shown in Figure 18.14.

```
# Select columns with numeric missing values
num_cols = ['age', 'bp', 'sg', 'al', 'su', 'bgr', 'bu', 'sc', 'sod', 'pot', 'hemo']
# Replace missing values with mean
for col in num_cols:
    data[col].fillna(data[col].mean(), inplace=True)

# Select columns with categorical missing values
cat_cols = ['rbc', 'pc', 'pcc', 'ba', 'pcv', 'wc', 'rc', 'htn', 'dm', 'cad', 'appet', 'pe', 'ane']
# Replace missing values using backfill
for col in cat_cols:
    data[col].fillna(method='backfill', inplace=True)

/home/u197692/tmp/ipykernel_3166024/84982855.py:6: FutureWarning: Series.fillna with 'method' is deprecated and will raise in a future version. Use obj.ffill() or obj.bfill() instead.
    data[col].fillna(method='backfill', inplace=True)
```

Figure 18.7 To replace the missing values.

```
[13]:  data.isnull().sum()
```

```
[13]:  age                0
       bp                 0
       sg                 0
       al                 0
       su                 0
       rbc                0
       pc                 0
       pcc                0
       ba                 0
       bgr                0
       bu                 0
       sc                 0
       sod                0
       pot                0
       hemo               0
       pcv                0
       wc                 0
       rc                 0
       htn                0
       dm                 0
       cad                0
       appet              0
       pe                 0
       ane                0
       classification     0
       dtype: int64
```

Figure 18.8 Replacing the missing values.

```
from sklearn.preprocessing import LabelEncoder
cat_cols = ['sg', 'al', 'su', 'rbc', 'pc', 'pcc', 'ba', 'htn', 'dm', 'cad', 'appet', 'pe', 'ane', 'classification']
# Create an instance of LabelEncoder
label_encoder = LabelEncoder()
# Encode categorical columns
for col in cat_cols:
    data[col] = label_encoder.fit_transform(data[col].astype(str))
```

Figure 18.9 Using LabelEncoder method.

```
[17]: data.head()
```

	age	bp	sg	al	su	rbc	pc	pcc	ba	bgr	...	pcv	wc	rc	htn	dm	cad	appet	pe	ane	classification
0	48.0	80.0	4	1	0	1	1	0	0	121.000000	...	44	7800	5.2	1	1	0	0	0	0	0
1	7.0	50.0	4	5	0	1	1	0	0	148.036517	...	38	6000	3.9	0	0	0	0	0	0	0
2	62.0	80.0	1	3	4	1	1	0	0	423.000000	...	31	7500	3.9	0	1	0	1	0	1	0
3	48.0	70.0	0	5	0	1	0	1	0	117.000000	...	32	6700	3.9	1	0	0	1	1	1	0
4	51.0	80.0	1	3	0	1	1	0	0	106.000000	...	35	7300	4.6	0	0	0	0	0	0	0

5 rows × 25 columns

Figure 18.10 Dataset after encoding.

```
import pandas as pd
from sklearn.model_selection import train_test_split
from sklearn.preprocessing import LabelEncoder
from sklearn.linear_model import LogisticRegression
from sklearn.svm import SVC
from sklearn.neighbors import KNeighborsClassifier
from sklearn.ensemble import RandomForestClassifier
from sklearn.metrics import accuracy_score, confusion_matrix
import matplotlib.pyplot as plt
import seaborn as sns

X = data.drop('classification', axis=1)
y = data['classification']
X_train, X_test, y_train, y_test = train_test_split(X, y, test_size=0.2, random_state=42)
```

Figure 18.11 Importing necessary libraries.

```
# Logistic Regression
lr = LogisticRegression()
lr.fit(X_train, y_train)
lr_pred = lr.predict(X_test)
lr_acc = accuracy_score(y_test, lr_pred)
lr_cm = confusion_matrix(y_test, lr_pred)
lr_acc
```

Figure 18.12 Initializing LR Classifier.

```
# SVM
svm = SVC()
svm.fit(X_train, y_train)
svm_pred = svm.predict(X_test)
svm_acc = accuracy_score(y_test, svm_pred)
svm_cm = confusion_matrix(y_test, svm_pred)
svm_acc
```

Figure 18.13 Initializing SVM Classifier.

```
knn = KNeighborsClassifier()
knn.fit(X_train, y_train)
knn_acc = knn.score(X_train, y_train)
print("KNN's Accuracy is: ", knn_acc)
```

Figure 18.14 Initializing KNN Classifier.

18.4 MODEL COMPARISON AND VISUALIZATION

We print the accuracy of our trained model. Logistic regression with 96.25% outperforms the other two models as illustrated in Figure 18.15.

In this section we import the matplotlib library for visualization. Then we define a list of accuracy values corresponding to each model. A bar graph is then initialized as in Figure 18.16 in which the x-axis represents the model names and the y-axis represents the accuracy values.

```
[26]: # Print accuracy for each model
      print("Logistic Regression Accuracy:", lr_acc)
      print("SVM Accuracy:", svm_acc)
      print("KNN Accuracy:", knn_acc)

      Logistic Regression Accuracy: 0.9625
      SVM Accuracy: 0.65
      KNN Accuracy: 0.828125
```

Figure 18.15 Accuracy comparison.

```
[27]: import matplotlib.pyplot as plt
      # Define the accuracy values for each model
      accuracy_values = [lr_acc,svm_acc,knn_acc]
      # Define the labels for each model
      model_labels = ['Logistic Regression', 'SVM', 'KNN']
      # Plot a bar graph
      plt.bar(model_labels, accuracy_values)
      # Add a title and labels to the plot
      plt.title('Accuracy Comparison of Different Models')
      plt.xlabel('Model')
      plt.ylabel('Accuracy')
      # Display the plot
      plt.show()
```

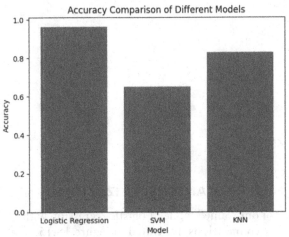

Figure 18.16 Bar graph comparison.

18.5 CONCLUSION

In summary, this study conducted a thorough examination of the renal illness dataset, encompassing the handling of missing values and the encoding of categorical variables. Subsequently, Logistic Regression, Support Vector Machine (SVM), and K-Nearest Neighbors (KNN) models were employed for the purpose of classification. The findings demonstrated favorable levels of accuracy: Logistic Regression reached a rate of 96.25%, SVM exhibited a rate of 65%, and KNN produced a rate of 82.81% accuracy on the test data.

18.6 FURTHER LEARNING

Possible improvements encompass the implementation of feature engineering techniques to capture intricate interactions, meticulous hyperparameter tuning, and comprehensive model evaluation that takes into account the metrics beyond accuracy. Feature selection approaches have the potential to improve the performance of models, while the investigation of ensemble techniques like Random Forest has the potential to augment prediction accuracy. Furthermore, the implementation of the most effective model in practical scenarios, along with continuous surveillance and the possibility of further training, remains crucial. Furthermore, the incorporation of model explainability methodologies could yield significant insights, hence guaranteeing the interpretability of forecasts in crucial fields such as healthcare. The pursuit of these potential areas of investigation has the potential to enhance the precision and dependability of renal disease prognostication.

SUGGESTED READING

Chandradas, A., 2021, September 20. 5 Methods to Check for NaN Values in Python. Medium. https://towardsdatascience.com/5-methods-to-check-for-nan-values-in-in-python-3f21ddd17eed?gi=8eb57dd2f95b

A deep dive into multiclass flower classification with ResNet and VGG16 using oneAPI

LEARNING OBJECTIVES

After reading this chapter, the reader shall be able to:

- Acquire the knowledge to classify wide range of flowers through deep learning.
- Utilize the pre-trained models ResNet and VGG16 to achieve classification accuracy.

19.1 INTRODUCTION

The classification of flowers, a fundamental topic within the field of computer vision, engrosses both researchers and admirers. This chapter delves into the realm of deep learning, with the objective of addressing the complex challenge of classifying a wide range of flowers. What is the primary area of our concentration? Leveraging two prominent contenders in the field of deep learning, namely ResNet and VGG16. By utilizing these pre-trained models, we initiate an engaging endeavor towards attaining accurate flower classification with a high level of precision. The available dataset taken from kaggle, www.kaggle.com/datasets/kausthubkannan/5-flower-types-classif ication-dataset/data, consists of the captivating floral species, namely Lilly, Lotus, Orchid, Sunflower, and Tulip. This not only renders our assignment scientifically engaging but also aesthetically wonderful.

19.2 DATA PREPARATION AND VISUALIZATION

We first import the opendatasets library, which will be used to download open source datasets directly from the internet as in Figure 19.1. Then the dataset link is pasted. Once after the authentication is done using the kaggle key, our dataset is successfully downloaded.

This code imports the OS and we import ImageDataGenerator from tensorflow keras library that allows us to perform real-time data

DOI: 10.1201/9781032676685-20

```
import opendatasets as od
import os

od.download("https://www.kaggle.com/datasets/kausthubkannan/5-flower-types-classification-dataset/data")

Please provide your Kaggle credentials to download this dataset. Learn more: http://bit.ly/kaggle-creds
Your Kaggle username:
  akshaybr
Your Kaggle Key:
  ................................
Downloading 5-flower-types-classification-dataset.zip to ./5-flower-types-classification-dataset
100%|██████████| 242M/242M [01:04<00:00, 3.92MB/s]
```

Figure 19.1 Importing the opendatasets library.

augmentation during the training period. The red colored pop-up of Figure 19.2 shows our code is optimized with oneAPI.

The path of our downloaded dataset is stores in a variable called data_ dir. Dimensions are specified for images which will be resized accordingly. The batch size for training is specified in a variable named batch_size and the same can be referred from Figure 19.3.

To have a look at some images from each class we declare a variable class_labels and map class indices to class names and retrieve one image from each class. Finally, all the images are displayed in a single row as depicted in Figure 19.4.

19.3 DATA PREPROCESSING AND AUGMENTATION

We configure the ImageDataGenerator with various inputs like rescale, zoom range etc. The validation_split splits the dataset to 20% validation and 80% training. To look at the number of different classes present we print all the categories. Refer to Figure 19.5 for the code snippet.

A generator object train_generator and validation_generator is created which will provide batches of augmented image data during training and validation period to our models.

To generate batches of augmented data from the directory datagen.flow_ from_directory() is used as seen from Figure 19.6 and then we specify the path to the data directory. We resize our input images to specific dimensions and declare batch size, class mode which in our case is categorical and subset is also declared.

Similarly, the validation_generator is created for the validation subset declaring all the similar parameters as provided in the code snippet of Figure 19.7.

19.4 MODEL BUILDING, COMPILATION AND TRAINING

For modeling, additional necessary libraries are imported. We first built our first model ResNet50 and compiled it with Adam optimizer and categorical

```
[4]: import os
     from tensorflow.keras.preprocessing.image import ImageDataGenerator

2023-10-27 09:56:36.200512: I tensorflow/tsl/cuda/cudart_stub.cc:28] Could not find cuda drivers on your machine, GPU will not be used.
2023-10-27 09:56:39.522448: I tensorflow/tsl/cuda/cudart_stub.cc:28] Could not find cuda drivers on your machine, GPU will not be used.
2023-10-27 09:56:39.531937: I tensorflow/core/platform/cpu_feature_guard.cc:182] This TensorFlow binary is optimized to use available CPU instructions in performance-critical operations.
To enable the following instructions: AVX2 AVX512F FMA, in other operations, rebuild TensorFlow with the appropriate compiler flags.
2023-10-27 09:57:03.562440: W tensorflow/compiler/tf2tensorrt/utils/py_utils.cc:38] TF-TRT Warning: Could not find TensorRT
```

Figure 19.2 To perform real time data augmentation.

```
[5]:   # Define data directory
       data_dir = "5-flower-types-classification-dataset/flower_images"

[6]:   # Define image dimensions and batch size
       img_width, img_height = 150, 150
       batch_size = 32
```

Figure 19.3 Path specification.

cross entropy loss function. We train the model for 10 epochs using both the training and validation generators. Refer to Figure 19.8 for the code snippet.

Similarly, we build the Vgg16 model with all input parameters as seen in Figure 19.9. The code snippet for compilation of the two models is provided in Figure 19.10.

The models' testing accuracies are evaluated using the evaluate() method on the validation data generator, which is shown in Figure 19.11.

19.5 MODEL EVALUATION AND VISUALIZATION

The testing accuracies of ResNet (Mirza et al., 2023) and VGG16 (Bakasa and Viriri, 2023) models are plotted using a bar graph as shown in Figure 19.12 for visual comparison. We create a list to store both our model names. Then the accuracies list is created where we store the testing accuracies of both our models. It is seen that the ResNet model exhibits superior performance with 81.10% of validation accuracy in comparison to the Vgg16 which has 75.30% of validation accuracy . This finding suggests that ResNet exhibits superior generalization performance on the validation dataset, implying its efficacy in collecting fundamental information for the task of flower categorization. Finally, the barplot is plotted.

19.6 CONCLUSION

Within the domain of floral classification, our models have achieved resounding success. ResNet and VGG16, employing deep learning methodologies, have successfully discerned intricate details of floral specimens, resulting in notable levels of precision. This chapter serves as evidence of the integration of sophisticated algorithms and the aesthetic qualities inherent in the natural world. The capacity of the models to differentiate between Lilly and Lotus, Orchid and Sunflower, and Tulip and their respective counterparts exemplifies the convergence of technology and floral artistry.

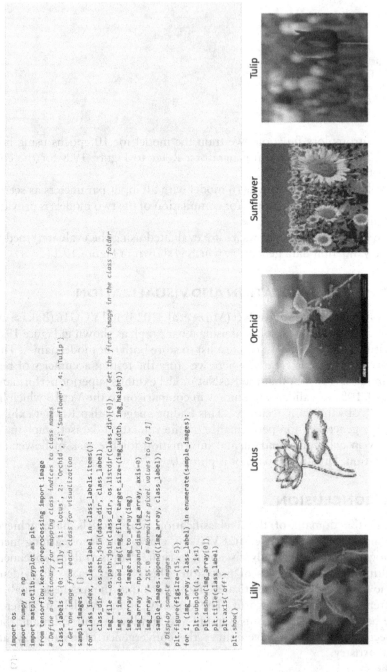

```
[7]: import os
import numpy as np
import matplotlib.pyplot as plt
from tensorflow.keras.preprocessing import image
# Define a dictionary for mapping class indices to class names
class_labels = {0: 'Lilly', 1: 'Lotus', 2: 'Orchid', 3: 'Sunflower', 4: 'Tulip'}
# Get one image from each class for visualization
sample_images = []
for class_index, class_label in class_labels.items():
    class_dir = os.path.join(data_dir, class_label)
    img_file = os.path.join(class_dir, os.listdir(class_dir)[0]) # Get the first image in the class folder
    img = image.load_img(img_file, target_size=(img_width, img_height))
    img_array = image.img_to_array(img)
    img_array = np.expand_dims(img_array, axis=0)
    img_array /= 255.0 # Normalize pixel values to [0, 1]
    sample_images.append((img_array, class_label))
# Display sample images
plt.figure(figsize=(15, 5))
for i, (img_array, class_label) in enumerate(sample_images):
    plt.subplot(1, 5, i+1)
    plt.imshow(img_array[0])
    plt.title(class_label)
    plt.axis('off')
plt.show()
```

Figure 19.4 To visualize images.

```
[7]:  # Data preprocessing and augmentation
      datagen = ImageDataGenerator(
          rescale=1.0/255.0,  # Normalize pixel values to [0, 1]
          shear_range=0.2,
          zoom_range=0.2,
          horizontal_flip=True,
          validation_split=0.2  # Split data into 80% training and 20% validation
      )
```

```
[10]:  categories = os.listdir(data_dir)
       print(categories)

       ['Lotus', 'Sunflower', 'Lilly', 'Orchid', 'Tulip']
```

Figure 19.5 Data Preprocessing and Augmentation.

```
[11]:  # Load and preprocess training data
       train_generator = datagen.flow_from_directory(
           data_dir,
           target_size=(img_width, img_height),
           batch_size=batch_size,
           class_mode='categorical',
           subset='training'  # Specify training data
       )

       Found 4000 images belonging to 5 classes.
```

Figure 19.6 Generating batches of augmented data.

```
[12]:  # Load and preprocess validation data
       validation_generator = datagen.flow_from_directory(
           data_dir,
           target_size=(img_width, img_height),
           batch_size=batch_size,
           class_mode='categorical',
           subset='validation'  # Specify validation data
       )

       Found 1000 images belonging to 5 classes.
```

Figure 19.7 To validate data.

```
[14]:  from tensorflow.keras.preprocessing.image import ImageDataGenerator
       from tensorflow.keras.applications import ResNet50, VGG16
       from tensorflow.keras.models import Model
       from tensorflow.keras.layers import Dense, GlobalAveragePooling2D
       import matplotlib.pyplot as plt
```

```
[15]:  # Build ResNet model
       resnet_model = ResNet50(weights='imagenet', include_top=False)
       x = resnet_model.output
       x = GlobalAveragePooling2D()(x)
       predictions_resnet = Dense(5, activation='softmax')(x)
       resnet_model_final = Model(inputs=resnet_model.input, outputs=predictions_resnet)
```

Figure 19.8 To Build ResNet model.

```
[16]:  # Build VGG16 model
       vgg16_model = VGG16(weights='imagenet', include_top=False)
       x = vgg16_model.output
       x = GlobalAveragePooling2D()(x)
       predictions_vgg16 = Dense(5, activation='softmax')(x)
       vgg16_model_final = Model(inputs=vgg16_model.input, outputs=predictions_vgg16)
```

Figure 19.9 To Build Vgg16 model.

19.7 FURTHER LEARNING

As we contemplate the future, multitudes of potentialities emerge. Engaging in the process of refining our models, investigating sophisticated architectures such as DenseNet and Inception, and delving into the realm of explainable AI present captivating opportunities. Moreover, the utilization of these models in practical contexts, such as the automation of flower identification in the field of horticulture, exhibits significant potential. The expedition does not conclude at this point; rather, it undergoes a metamorphosis, enticing us into unexplored frontiers inside the continuously developing realm of deep learning.

```
[17]:  # Compile models
       resnet_model_final.compile(optimizer='adam', loss='categorical_crossentropy', metrics=['accuracy'])
       vgg16_model_final.compile(optimizer='adam', loss='categorical_crossentropy', metrics=['accuracy'])
```

Figure 19.10 To compile models.

```
# Compare testing accuracy
resnet_test_accuracy = resnet_model_final.evaluate(validation_generator, verbose=0)[1]
vgg16_test_accuracy = vgg16_model_final.evaluate(validation_generator, verbose=0)[1]
```

Figure 19.11 To calculate accuracies.

```
[23]:   # Create a bar graph
        models = ['ResNet', 'VGG16']
        accuracies = [resnet_test_accuracy, vgg16_test_accuracy]

        plt.bar(models, accuracies, color=['blue', 'orange'])
        plt.ylabel('Testing Accuracy')
        plt.title('Comparison of Testing Accuracy')
        plt.ylim(0, 1)  # Set y-axis limit to 0-1 for accuracy percentage
        plt.show()
```

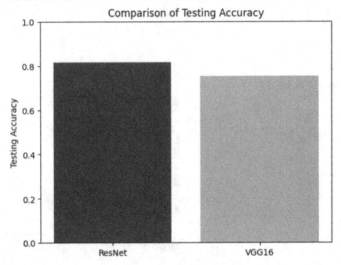

Figure 19.12 For model evaluation and visualization.

SUGGESTED READINGS

Bakasa, W. and Viriri, S., 2023. Vgg16 feature extractor with extreme gradient boost classifier for pancreas cancer prediction. *Journal of Imaging, 9*(7), p.138.

Mirza, A.F., Mansoor, M., Usman, M. and Ling, Q., 2023. Hybrid Inception-embedded deep neural network ResNet for short and medium-term PV-Wind forecasting. *Energy Conversion and Management, 294*, 117574.

Chapter 20

Dive into **X** (formerly Twitter's) emotions using oneAPI

Sentiment analysis with NLP

LEARNING OBJECTIVES

By the end of this chapter, the reader shall be able to:

- Acquire the knowledge to assess thoughts with deep learning capabilities.
- Examine fundamental approaches in Natural Language Processing to design a robust deep learning model.

20.1 INTRODUCTION

In the contemporary era of digital technology, possessing the ability to comprehend and interpret human emotions as sent through internet platforms holds immense significance and worth. Sentiment analysis, an essential application of Natural Language Processing (NLP), enables the interpretation of sentiment expressed in textual data. This chapter initiates an engaging exploration, employing the capabilities of deep learning to assess thoughts expressed on the Twitter platform with a dataset extracted from Kaggle: www.kaggle.com/datasets/kazanova/sentiment140. In this study, we will examine fundamental approaches in Natural Language Processing (NLP), explore complex preprocessing methods, design a resilient deep learning model, and accurately decipher feelings.

20.2 INSIGHTS AND PREPROCESSING TECHNIQUES IN NATURAL LANGUAGE PROCESSING (NLP)

Natural Language Processing (NLP) is an interdisciplinary domain that integrates the fields of linguistics, computer science, and artificial intelligence (AI). Preprocessing is a crucial stage in natural language processing (NLP) that serves to improve the quality of data and facilitate the model's comprehension. Within our repertoire of preprocessing techniques:

- **Text Cleaning:** The process of cleaning raw Twitter data typically involves removing URLs, mentions, and hashtags, as they tend to clutter the data. The process of cleaning entails the removal of these artifacts, so assuring that the model is directed exclusively towards the textual essence.
- **Tokenization:** Tokenization refers to the process of breaking down language into its constituent units, known as words, which serve as the fundamental building blocks of linguistic communication. Tokenization is a process that involves breaking down textual data into individual words or sub words, to establish a structured format that facilitates analysis.
- **Padding and sequencing:** These are essential techniques in the context of neural networks, as they address the requirement for fixed-length inputs. The inclusion of padding in a dataset facilitates the achievement of consistency, hence enhancing the effectiveness of batch processing during the training phase. The process of sequencing involves the transformation of linguistic units into numerical representations, rendering them suitable for computational analysis using machine learning methods.
- **Word embeddings:** Words possess intricate relationships. Word embeddings are a type of computational representation that convert words into vectors with a large number of dimensions. These vectors are designed to capture the semantic meanings and contextual nuances associated with the words. This modification improves the model's comprehension of lexical relationships.

The dataset we are going to use is obtained from Kaggle using the opendatasets library. For handling the csv data, we import the pandas library as seen in Figure 20.1.

Next we store our dataset in a variable called df. As we are handling categorical values, we declare special parameters like encoding = "latin" which will handle special characters. As we look at our dataset the first column is our target column. See Figure 20.2.

For better understanding and accessibility, let us give our columns the actual names from the information obtained from the Kaggle website as shown in Figure 20.3.

```
import pandas as pd

import opendatasets as od
od.download("https://www.kaggle.com/datasets/kazanova/sentiment140/data")
```

Figure 20.1 Importing the libraries.

```
# Load your dataset
df = pd.read_csv("sentiment140/training.1600000.processed.noemoticon.csv",encoding = 'latin',header=None)

df.head()
```

	0	1	2	3	4	5
0	0	1467810369	Mon Apr 06 22:19:45 PDT 2009	NO_QUERY	_TheSpecialOne_	@switchfoot http://twitpic.com/2y1zl - Awww, t...
1	0	1467810672	Mon Apr 06 22:19:49 PDT 2009	NO_QUERY	scotthamilton	is upset that he can't update his Facebook by ...
2	0	1467810917	Mon Apr 06 22:19:53 PDT 2009	NO_QUERY	mattycus	@Kenichan I dived many times for the ball. Man...
3	0	1467811184	Mon Apr 06 22:19:57 PDT 2009	NO_QUERY	ElleCTF	my whole body feels itchy and like its on fire
4	0	1467811193	Mon Apr 06 22:19:57 PDT 2009	NO_QUERY	Karoli	@nationwideclass no, it's not behaving at all....

Figure 20.2 Loading the dataset.

```
df.columns = ['sentiment', 'id', 'date', 'query', 'user_id', 'text']
df.head()
```

	sentiment	id	date	query	user_id	text
0	0	1467810369	Mon Apr 06 22:19:45 PDT 2009	NO_QUERY	_TheSpecialOne_	@switchfoot http://twitpic.com/2y1zl - Awww, t...
1	0	1467810672	Mon Apr 06 22:19:49 PDT 2009	NO_QUERY	scotthamilton	is upset that he can't update his Facebook by ...
2	0	1467810917	Mon Apr 06 22:19:53 PDT 2009	NO_QUERY	mattycus	@Kenichan I dived many times for the ball. Man...
3	0	1467811184	Mon Apr 06 22:19:57 PDT 2009	NO_QUERY	ElleCTF	my whole body feels itchy and like its on fire
4	0	1467811193	Mon Apr 06 22:19:57 PDT 2009	NO_QUERY	Karoli	@nationwideclass no, it's not behaving at all....

Figure 20.3 To impart clarity.

Now we are dropping all our unwanted columns like "id," "query," "date," and '

"user_id." Then we map the unique values present in the column sentiment that is 0 and 4 with Negative and Positive respectively as provided in Figure 20.4.

20.3 TEXT CLEANING AND TOKENIZATION

We first import the necessary libraries needed for text cleaning, padding, and tokenization. The Regular Expression (regex) module is also imported as seen from Figure 20.5 which will allow us to do text manipulation. Then we clean the text which removes URLs, multiple spaces, hashtags etc.

A histogram is plotted to find the maximum sequence length as depicted in Figure 20.6. The sequence length variable will calculate the length of each sequence in the list "X." By observing the graph, it is seen around 10.0, so we can assign 10 as our maxlen.

Tokenization is performed by declaring the tokenizer class as illustrated in Figure 20.7. The num words specify the maximum number of unique words to tokenize and outside limit words are marked as <0OV>. Then the

```
df = df.drop(['id', 'date', 'query', 'user_id'], axis=1)
```

```
map_sentiment = {0:"Negative", 4:"Positive"}
def label_decoder(label):
  return map_sentiment[label]
df.sentiment = df.sentiment.apply(lambda x: label_decoder(x))
df.head(5)
```

	sentiment	text
0	Negative	@switchfoot http://twitpic.com/2y1zl - Awww, t...
1	Negative	is upset that he can't update his Facebook by ...
2	Negative	@Kenichan I dived many times for the ball. Man...
3	Negative	my whole body feels itchy and like its on fire
4	Negative	@nationwideclass no, it's not behaving at all....

Figure 20.4 Dropping unwanted columns.

```
import re
from tensorflow.keras.preprocessing.text import Tokenizer
from tensorflow.keras.preprocessing.sequence import pad_sequences
```

```
# Text cleaning function
def clean_text(text):
    text = re.sub(r'http\S+|www\S+|https\S+', '', text, flags=re.MULTILINE)
    text = re.sub(r'\s+', ' ', text, flags=re.MULTILINE)
    text = re.sub(r'\@\w+|\#', '', text)
    return text
```

Figure 20.5 For text cleaning.

texts are converted into sequences and padded to maintain the same length. In this case, the sequences are padded to a maximum length of 10 based on the histogram plot mentioned earlier.

We import and initialize OneHotEncoder as in Figure 20.8 to reshape our sentiment column into a 2-D array structure. After this operation, the y variable contains the one-hot encoded representation of the "sentiment" column. The red colored pop-up indicates that our code has been optimized with oneAPI for improved performance.

```
import matplotlib.pyplot as plt

# Calculate sequence lengths
sequence_lengths = [len(seq) for seq in X]

# Plot a histogram of sequence lengths
plt.hist(sequence_lengths, bins=50)
plt.xlabel('Sequence Length')
plt.ylabel('Frequency')
plt.show()
```

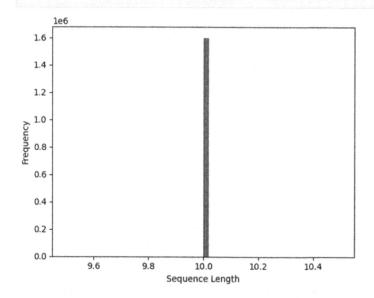

Figure 20.6 Histogram Plotting.

```
# Apply text cleaning
df['text'] = df['text'].apply(clean_text)

# Tokenization
max_words = 10000  # Number of unique words to tokenize
tokenizer = Tokenizer(num_words=max_words, oov_token='<OOV>')
tokenizer.fit_on_texts(df['text'])

# Convert text to sequences
X = tokenizer.texts_to_sequences(df['text'])
X = pad_sequences(X, maxlen=10)  # Max len based on plot
```

Figure 20.7 Tokenization.

```
from sklearn.preprocessing import OneHotEncoder

# One-hot encode sentiments
encoder = OneHotEncoder(sparse=False)
y = encoder.fit_transform(df['sentiment'].values.reshape(-1, 1))
```

```
Intel(R) Extension for Scikit-learn* enabled (https://github.com/intel/scikit-learn-intelex)
/opt/intel/oneapi/intelpython/latest/lib/python3.9/site-packages/sklearn/preprocessing/_encoders.py:868: FutureWarning: `sparse` was renamed to `sparse_output` in version 1.2 and will be removed in 1.4. `sparse_outp
ut` is ignored unless you leave `sparse` to its default value.
  warnings.warn(
```

Figure 20.8 Initializing OneHotEncoder.

20.4 MODEL BUILDING, COMPILATION, AND TRAINING

A Neural network model is then created using keras for classifying the texts. We use a sequential model that has a linear stack of layers. First, an embedding layer is used to convert integers into dense vectors, followed by an LSTM (Long Short-Term Memory) layer capable of learning long-term dependencies. Finally, the output layer for binary classification is used. The model is then compiled with Adam optimizer.

The data is now split into training and testing sets as seen in Figure 20.9 and is fitted for training.

Evaluating the model on testing data is seen to achieve an accuracy of 79.85%, as evident from Figure 20.10.

We utilize the trained model for the purpose of generating predictions on new data, namely new_texts. The text sequences should be tokenized and padded before utilizing the model for sentiment label prediction. The function encoder.inverse_transform is employed to reverse the encoding process and convert the predicted values back to their original labels. The anticipated classifications are displayed as the resulting output (refer to Figures 20.11 and 20.12).

20.5 CONCLUSION

The present study involved the processing and utilization of a X (formerly known as Twitter) sentiment analysis dataset obtained from Kaggle. The dataset was employed to construct a resilient sentiment analysis model utilizing LSTM neural networks. The dataset underwent preprocessing procedures that involved many steps. Firstly, the sentiment values were mapped to the categories of "Negative" and "Positive." Secondly, the text data was cleaned by eliminating URLs and special characters. Lastly, the text was tokenized into numerical sequences and padded accordingly. The dataset consisted of various columns including "sentiment," "id," "date," "query," "user_id," and "text." Subsequently, a Long Short-Term Memory (LSTM) model was developed, comprising an embedding layer to represent words, an LSTM layer to capture sequential patterns, and a dense output layer for the purpose of binary classification. The model underwent training using preprocessed data, resulting in significant accuracy improvements over multiple epochs. Finally, the model effectively made accurate predictions regarding feelings for novel textual instances, showcasing its practicality in the context of sentiment analysis tasks in real-world scenarios.

20.6 FURTHER LEARNING

The current investigation focused on the processing and utilization of a dataset for Twitter sentiment analysis, which was acquired from Kaggle. The

```
from tensorflow.keras.models import Sequential
from tensorflow.keras.layers import Embedding, LSTM, Dense

embedding_dim = 128
lstm_units = 64

model = Sequential()
model.add(Embedding(input_dim=max_words, output_dim=embedding_dim, input_length=10))
model.add(LSTM(units=lstm_units))
model.add(Dense(units=2, activation='softmax'))  # 2 output units for binary classification (Negative and Positive)

model.compile(optimizer='adam', loss='categorical_crossentropy', metrics=['accuracy'])
```

Figure 20.9 Model creation.

```
from sklearn.model_selection import train_test_split

# Split data into training and testing sets
X_train, X_test, y_train, y_test = train_test_split(X, y, test_size=0.2, random_state=42)

# Train the model
model.fit(X_train, y_train, epochs=5, batch_size=64, validation_split=0.1)

Epoch 1/5
18000/18000 [==============================] - 257s 14ms/step - loss: 0.4523 - accuracy: 0.7849 - val_loss: 0.4369 - val_accuracy: 0.7968
Epoch 2/5
18000/18000 [==============================] - 254s 14ms/step - loss: 0.4162 - accuracy: 0.8059 - val_loss: 0.4257 - val_accuracy: 0.8017
Epoch 3/5
18000/18000 [==============================] - 254s 14ms/step - loss: 0.3957 - accuracy: 0.8178 - val_loss: 0.4264 - val_accuracy: 0.8025
Epoch 4/5
18000/18000 [==============================] - 255s 14ms/step - loss: 0.3769 - accuracy: 0.8286 - val_loss: 0.4318 - val_accuracy: 0.8006
Epoch 5/5
18000/18000 [==============================] - 253s 14ms/step - loss: 0.3581 - accuracy: 0.8389 - val_loss: 0.4408 - val_accuracy: 0.7972
<keras.src.callbacks.History at 0x7eff4c7604f0>
```

Figure 20.10 Dataset splitting.

```
[27]: # Evaluate the model
      loss, accuracy = model.evaluate(X_test, y_test)
      print(f'Test Loss: {loss:.2f}')
      print(f'Test Accuracy: {accuracy*100:.2f}%')

      10000/10000 [==============================] - 43s 4ms/step - loss: 0.4383 - accuracy: 0.7985
      Test Loss: 0.44
      Test Accuracy: 79.85%
```

Figure 20.11 Model evaluation.

```
# Example: Make predictions on new data
new_texts = ["I love this product!", "This movie is terrible."]
new_sequences = tokenizer.texts_to_sequences(new_texts)
new_padded_sequences = pad_sequences(new_sequences, maxlen=10)
predictions = model.predict(new_padded_sequences)

# Decode predictions
predicted_labels = encoder.inverse_transform(predictions)
print(predicted_labels)

1/1 [==============================] - 0s 495ms/step
[['Positive']
 ['Negative']]
```

Figure 20.12 Generating Predictions on new data.

dataset was utilized for the purpose of constructing a robust sentiment analysis model by employing LSTM neural networks. The dataset underwent a
series of preprocessing operations that encompassed multiple steps. Initially,
the sentiment values were assigned to the respective categories of "Negative"
and "Positive." Furthermore, the text data underwent a cleaning process
wherein URLs and unusual characters were removed. Finally, the text
underwent tokenization to convert it into numerical sequences, which were
then appropriately padded. The dataset comprised several columns, namely
"sentiment," "id," "date," "query," "user_id," and "text." Following this,
a Long Short-Term Memory (LSTM) model was constructed, consisting
of an embedding layer to encode word representations, an LSTM layer to
record sequential patterns, and a dense output layer for binary classification. The model was subjected to a training process utilizing preprocessed
data, which led to notable enhancements in accuracy across many epochs.
Ultimately, the model successfully generated precise predictions pertaining
to emotions for unfamiliar textual examples, so demonstrating its usefulness
within the realm of sentiment analysis applications in real-life situations.

Index

Printed in the United States
by Baker & Taylor Publisher Services